917.2
S.55c

WITHDRAWN

The Changing Wind

THE
CHANGING
WIND

by Karena Shields

Thomas Y. Crowell Company

NEW YORK · ESTABLISHED 1834

To My Mother and Father

and all those who made San Leandro memorable

Foreword

I

T WAS HERE, in San Leandro's quiet living, that I came to know the meaning of things. Here the earth from which we are born first spoke aloud to me. Here I first knew that I moved and breathed and had freedom to look out for myself and back at myself. Here I discovered that the moon is sometimes a satellite and sometimes made of green cheese.

Memory is a curious thing. For some, all of childhood is one continuous stretch of happenings, blurred and indistinct in the mind except for large griefs or occasions of tremendous change. For others, as for me, everything remains clear to the smallest detail, for I had a photographic memory and an ability to identify myself with everything I saw, with everything others felt. So experiences claimed me, and I became a part of every scene rather than a mere passer-by. I was one with the horses running in the pasture; I knew the texture and color of a leaf not merely as something touched and seen but as something deeply experienced and shared. To me all days were different, all things that happened were new and sharp and not to be forgotten.

This book is a record of how I lived in those days, of what I learned about life everywhere while growing up in a wild jungle world.

K.S.

Finca Tacalapán de San Leandro
Chiapas, Mexico

Part I

I FIRST CAME to San Leandro on the back of a Chamula. His skin was the color of a red clay olla, his hair grew in a straight black thatch on his head, and his eyes were dark and piercing. His name was Bartolo. I couldn't understand a word he said, but he looked at me and smiled a warm, friendly sort of smile full of white, even Indian teeth, and I knew at once that to ride on his shoulders would be all right.

A chairlike contrivance had been arranged in a rectangular box, with a cushion and a curtain that could be lifted or lowered, and this was my palanquin. It was carried on Bartolo's back, held in place by a tumpline, a heavy leather band across his forehead that pulled my weight against his neck and shoulder muscles. When the other Chamulas who were to carry our trunks and boxes put leather bands on their foreheads and swung the luggage onto their backs as if the heavy things were toys, I understood well enough how I was to travel.

Bartolo was stocky and not very tall, but in my chair I swayed above everything and thought the ground quite

3

far below. He walked carefully for my sake, using a swift, bent-kneed swing that made the steepest trails smooth. At first I lurched along like a camel-driver, but after a little got used to the swaying motion and peeked out from behind my curtain with less dizziness and more curiosity.

I was a very little girl, but there is an advantage in being three-going-on-four. The whole world is a bit new, and whatever comes is accepted as the way things are. My box chair, surprising at first, soon came to seem quite a normal method of travel.

We had started this last leg of our journey into the jungle well before dawn, sitting cramped in a narrow dugout all the way up the Tulija River, which was wide and deep and green-blue, and then into the Michol, which was narrow and deep and dark. At Moctezuma, on the Michol, horses were waiting from the finca San Leandro, the rubber plantation of which Father was the newly appointed manager.

Father, Mother, and my sister were to ride horseback. I was envious at first, but Father made my palanquin appear better after all.

"There is an advantage in going backward," he said. "We will see things before they come, but you will see them afterward and can look at them longer." This was such a new idea that my head came up, my eyes wide and looking out. So I saw everything there was to see along the narrow jungle trail.

The tropical forest spread above my head, and dank leaves crowded in against the trail, smelling strong of green life. The jungle was a welcoming host of silent living things, but there was something else too, though I could not have said what it was. It was something that curled itself around my sense of being and cradled me in a warm

4

silence. It had to do with the darkness and the light that sifted down from above on all the pungent greenness about us. It had to do with the immenseness of the forest, and an expectancy as if some great secret lay here and would reveal itself if we could only see.

There are those who say that my coming to this place backward made a difference in what was to happen. And there are some who say that it was because we came at the end of the fifty-second week of the Mayan calendar. And of course there is always someone to talk of destiny. As for me, I do not know. I only felt the hunger that was born in me, and looked for something I could not remember, and waited for those moments when God put His face down close to mine, as He does to most children at some time in their lives. On that first morning, as we started on the winding jungle trail, I was certainly not thinking of change or of what was to happen.

Father rode ahead. High adventure gave his blue eyes a deep-sea color, a characteristic of his that gave his plain, squarish face and straight sandy hair a vital and arresting quality. He turned back from time to time to check us all, and a king on a white charger could not have looked more powerful and noble to me. Under his cork helmet his blue eyes flashed at me above his reddish beard. I was enchanted with him, and each time he left me I squirmed around to watch him ride away, longing to have him lift me onto his saddle so that I might go proudly in front.

Mother rode behind me to see that I did not fall out, admonishing me gently from time to time if I leaned out too far to stare up at the wild flight of parrots or toucans. Mother was small and dark, and everything about her was elegant in a delicate way. Her starched white shirtwaist,

5

her neat divided skirt of fine material (concession to the new unorthodox jungle life), her fringed gauntlets and soft Panama "riding hat" worn at a becoming angle, were correct in every way. The deep mud, heavy wet foliage, and high-backed Mexican saddle were a far cry from the parks and lanes and American riding gear to which she was accustomed.

Lucia, older than I and therefore privileged to ride her own horse, had a dignity that I envied greatly. She was seven, a slim little girl with large brown eyes and blond hair and a serious, thoughtful way. I thought her quite beautiful. Her quiet manner covered a wildly imaginative and dramatic interior being who took my simple, forthright world in magic fingers and turned most things into breathtaking and amazing experiences. She could read, and what things she read to me! To me the world was exciting, but all things were quite regular and were not in the least strange. Lucia, her big brown eyes alight, shifted the prosaic out of focus and turned it into a horrendous and fascinating reality. I did not know what she was thinking of the jungle and the journey, but once she winked at me knowingly, and immediately the woods became full of an Arthur Rackham sort of wooshiness, and I retired behind the curtain to be very mysterious and still and to wait until whatever it was she had conjured up had passed. That I really thought Lucia was a superior being who knew all about the world in a most mystic way there is no doubt, and certainly she took delight in using her quick imagination to create for me and make me the dutiful slave I was.

It never occurred to me to doubt the validity of Lucia's "pretends," and we entered into a world of our own making each time the knowing wink was given. But this time, in these new woods, I shrank from the wink. There was something else here, and I wanted to know about it on my own. Perhaps this was my first rejection of a pretend world, but I did not know it.

We stopped at a strange dark place of thatched huts built on stilts near a murky river that had flooded and left bare mud banks. Mother told me to keep my curtain down because there were clouds of mosquitoes, but I peered out to see naked children with swollen stomachs and great dark eyes that stared back at me. We had to cross the river in a dugout, and Bartolo stepped in, chair and me and all, squatted on his heels in the narrow canoe, and rested the chair on the gunwale. I could see dark swirling water that lapped almost at my feet, and I heard the droning chant of the man who poled the canoe as he called out to the horses swimming alongside to give them courage. One little colt, plunging desperately behind his mother, put his chin up on her rump and paddled behind her, successfully keeping his nose out of water. Mother, in a canoe behind us, kept saying, "Oh, the little horse, he will drown." But she said it in English, so no one understood her.

At the far bank we nosed smoothly into the mud and reeds. But the horses, lunging up, almost tipped us over and threw water all over our saddles and Mother's clean shirtwaist. She smiled and sponged it off, patting Papa's arm when he looked sorry, but I knew how she hated to be the least bit mussed.

On the far side of the river the forest changed. We were now entering high hills, the beginning of a mountain range. We couldn't tell how far up we were because the jungle was dense and towered high over us; we couldn't see the treetops, even with squinting eyes and heads thrown clear

7

back. But the high rain-forest jungle—that is, mountain jungle—had characteristics very different from low jungle or "bush." A tree was no longer a single tree, but several sprouting one from the other. Parasites sprang out of the upper branches of mahogany and ceiba, and lianas hung down in great curtains of leaves and spiny tendrils. It was here that we began to see monkeys shrieking through the branches, leaning down hand over tail to snatch at twigs just above our heads, and chattering at us in rage and surprise. Once macaws flew close, great splashes of gaudy color, wild creatures of a wild place, the very extravagance of them part of a new feeling that grew until we were at the gates of San Leandro itself.

San Leandro had been prepared for us; Father had seen to that on a preliminary visit. For our coming the grass and brush had been cleared from the fenced-in acres of garden, and in this process twenty-seven nauyacas, deadly bushmasters, had been found and killed. Following tradition, the snakes had been skinned and their bodies coiled on pyres to be burned, leaving little smoldering piles to mark the death of "evil." The long, diamond-marked, gray-brown skins hanging in limp rows on drying poles were the first things we saw; they were just outside the great gate of the finca, traditionally not allowed inside the compound until the sun had taken all semblance of life away. It was a strange omen to greet us, and Mother turned her face away and called our attention to a cascade of red blossoms by the gate. But except for some of the Chamulas who trotted rapidly past without looking, busily crossing themselves, no one really thought much of it beyond the first surprise.

Arriving backward, as I did, I saw the finca village unfold behind me—first the big gate with its heavy beams closed and locked, then the widening grass of the village,

8

the small thatched houses in two neat rows on each side with families standing there to greet us. They wore spotless white and blue, the colors of the Bachajón, Chol, and Tzeltal tribes. An occasional bright pink or green rebozo flaunted across the head and shoulders of a ladino's wife. Two hundred families in all stood there, chickens and children running in the thick green close-cropped grass, dogs barking with the high shrill screaming bark of the red dog of these hills. In the center of the village was a stone platform with a small kiosk over it, where orchestras performed on feast days. Our coming was a feast day for all, and as our cavalcade rode past the kiosk a five-man band started up, beating out thunderous uneven Indian rhythms on drums, flutes, maracas, and a ponderous harplike instrument that echoed with a deep contralto.

I was fascinated, staring into the peoples' faces and being stared at, wondering at the small children who suddenly stopped, naked and unafraid, to wonder back at me. All the people were clean and neat; the little gardens beside each house were neat; the orange trees and the tall coconut palms that lined the wide grassy street were set in rows like ninepins, each just so far from the other. Then on one side came corrals with horses and mules looking over the fences, and on the other side a large cement platform with tiled roof and no walls, where tanks and vats and other rubber-curing equipment awaited production. And then Bartolo set me down on the cement walk that led up a slight rise to our garden gate, Mother loosened my safety belt and lifted me out, and I stood uncertainly in the bright sunlight, looking for the first time at the half-mile expanse of the village and the jungle-covered hills that ringed it round.

The smells of burning charcoal and grass still wet from

9

the afternoon shower, the ever present leaf-mold odor of the jungle, and the heavy sweetness of flowering trees and bushes were first impressions that dug deep into my mind and left me standing, heart in mouth, in a kind of wonder. Mother tugged at me and laughed at the round-eyed stillness that possessed me, but it wasn't until the village families moved toward us, happiness in their faces, respect in their manner, and curiosity in their voices, that I was able to lift my feet and turn toward the house. The people came on, surrounding us on the walk by the gate, bright sashes around the white trousers of the men, dark rebozos pulled over the heads of the Tzeltal women. They held these scarfs across their faces so that only their eyes received the newcomers, their full skirts swishing against their ankles, their arms holding up babies and small children for my father's blessing and my mother's smile.

The garden gate swung open, and beyond a big bread-fruit tree, orange trees, and flowering frangipani, the house waited. Standing in the screened doorway was Charlie Ah Fong, the Chinese cook, in black silk suit and long queue, his hands folded in front of him, his eyes squinted into welcoming slits. He seemed pleased to have a family again.

So we stood, the four of us, on the threshold of this new place, in one of those moments of silent recognition before the action of moving forward into it begins. We looked about us at the tropical world and the strangely dressed people, each with his own feelings and forebodings, his own sense of surprise and pleasure. With what mixed emotions Mother may have first looked upon the place I can only surmise, but in spite of her tremendous weariness, the unaccustomed trails and saddles, the welcome she found

10

was a good one. She was now La Señora, queen of this place, to be looked up to, admired as the señora of Don Guillermo, and well guarded in all that was to come. Even I, miniature human, sensed that relatively I had changed stature and was now in a position of responsibility and authority before all these people who were so different from me but so beautiful in my eyes. They moved like palm trees in a soft wind, their voices were low and warm, their eyes looked at mine with laughter and gentleness; and suddenly it was very good to be here among them. I glanced quickly at Lucia in these moments of "presentation" to our villagers and workers, but she had a remote, lofty look that closed her away with a "no comment" expression. As always, I thought she looked like a princess royal, and humbly I tried to stand up straighter, pulling my plump arms tight to my body and standing squarely on my pudgy legs while Father made his speech of welcome to the people. Then we turned and went through the gate, up the flower-bordered walk to the house.

There it stood, long and low under a tile roof, much as the previous manager had left it. It had four bedrooms and a large, airy main room that went through the center of the building and had neither front nor back walls, only heavy curtains that could be drawn against strong wind or driving rain. A deep screened veranda surrounded the entire structure. The kitchen was in a separate building at the rear, as most kitchens are in the tropics, and there were other outbuildings too—a bathhouse, chicken coops in their own enclosures, and a small structure that would serve as Father's storeroom and office. Bright flowers and trees strange to us dotted the grass all around, and far away, beyond jumbled foothills, a great mountain reared its

11

bulk into the sky. This was, I felt, a good sort of place in which to live.

That first night was filled with plenty. The big mahogany table was covered with a white cloth, and there were platters of meat and chicken, rice piled high in bowls, and hot biscuits made specially for our homecoming. We sat looking at each other in the lamplight, our things still unpacked, tired and content after the long day. Charlie's smiling face watched us from the fringe of darkness just beyond the lamp on the table; Sabatán, the shuffling Indian houseboy, was hurrying back and forth with another biscuit or another glass of water, refilling my father's coffee cup; and we began to laugh out of sheer delight at having come to this place after all.

For suddenly there was nothing strange about where we were. All the things we had known elsewhere receded into an unreality beyond the black, starlit horizon that was so visible from where we sat. The night wind sifted through our house, lapping gently at the lamplight; sweet with wild vanilla and damp earth, it came down from the great jungled mountain that seemed so friendly behind us. As we ate dinner we could see, down in the village, the light of low fires where the people gathered in little knots to talk in the night, telling tales of past and future. They sang too, mostly in low voices, but sometimes a high falsetto soared up and away to the hills. It was a music that spoke clearly to me, and after dinner I sat quietly for a long time, curled in a string hammock on the porch, looking out into the dark warmth of the tropic night.

12

PEOPLE LEAVE their home places and go wandering to the far corners of the earth for many reasons—for adventure, for gain, for escape from failure or oppression or just plain boredom. My father came to this primeval jungle in southernmost Mexico for none of these purposes, but to build a good life according to his own ideas.

Nothing in his background suggested that he would do such a thing. William David Plant came of sturdy New England stock, and his early years showed little departure from the accepted American pattern of the time. He attended Amherst College and the University of Michigan, graduating from the latter in 1891. As an undergraduate he lived fully and eagerly in the usual collegiate fashion of the day, but always correctly, never unduly risking his puritanical father's disapproval. He pulled a strong oar in the crew, played football in the chrysanthemum haircut of the "gay nineties," belonged to the debating team, owned a sailboat and an iceboat, and was a member in good standing of Delta Upsilon fraternity. He was popular with

13

the girls too, taking three or four lovelies to every dance, seeing that their cards were filled, and always having one with whom to sit out, drink punch, and look at the moon— for an injured knee made dancing impossible for him.

When he married pretty Jeannie Jenkins a few years later and became president of a land company in Lorain, Ohio, it seemed that his way of life was set in the conventional mold—especially after Lucia and I had appeared on the scene. But other ideas had been germinating in him for years, and only the occasion was needed to bring them to fruition.

Those other ideas, individual and even adventurous, came in part from his mother's memories of covered-wagon days, in part from his uncle Edwin Heath's tales of the Beni River in Bolivia, which he had been the first to explore. But more important by far were the stimulating comradeships he formed at the university, in particular those with two outstanding men. One of these was John Dewey, then professor of philosophy at Michigan, and then as always no blind follower of tradition for its own sake. The other was Pierre du Pont, classmate and companion-in-argument in many an all-night session of what today might be called a discussion group. Here students and professors met to enjoy the stimulation of mental fisticuffs, to explore in endless argument the meaning of the universe and man's place in it, to settle and unsettle the eternal verities, in the unchanging fashion of live-minded undergraduates everywhere.

Out of these nights of query, reinforced in later years by much quiet reading and much profound thought, my father came to a determination to live as he thought a man was meant to live: to build a kingdom of his own, to taste

14

life fully and freely, and if need be to go to the ends of the earth to do it. He was not running away from anything or trying to prove anything. He was certainly not seeking security, for he was one who found his greatest security in a freedom that had in it no "security" at all—an open road, an unknown wilderness where he could do as he pleased, provided it was done with courtesy and he hadn't forgotten to raise his hat to the spirits that dwelt there.

The time came when intention and opportunity met. Some ten years after his marriage, Father came home one day with a pronouncement. He had been offered a position as manager of a rubber property in the jungle hinterlands of Chiapas, bordering on the Guatemalan highlands, and he had accepted it. And thus in one morning the lives of all of us—my mother, my sister, and me—were changed profoundly and forever.

Of course his decision startled and outraged our relatives and most of our friends, and they said so to Mother, quite vehemently. But for her there was no question of what to do. Her husband was going to Mexico, so she and the children were going too, and she said so quietly but with a characteristic firm tilt of her head. Although our relatives were quite possessive, even domineering, and had decided ideas on this subject, they knew it was useless to argue with Mother when she spoke in that way. So it was settled; Father would go and prepare the place for us, then come back and take us south.

The property to be under his charge belonged to a California corporation, the Chiapas Rubber Plantation and Investment Company. In those late days of the Díaz administration, Mexico was full of projects of the same character—agricultural or mining concessions of one sort or another whose main purpose was to float stock and bond issues for the quick enrichment of foreign promoters and Mexican officials. But that aspect of the matter never occurred to Father. He believed in this enterprise, he put his own money into it, and he set out to produce rubber and live his life as he wished it to be in that faraway spot where few civilized men had dwelt since the end of the Mayan empire a thousand years earlier.

So Father went away on a preliminary visit, and came back, and it was time for us to leave the town where we had been born on the shore of Lake Erie. We journeyed zigzag across the United States to California and Texas, and then down the world—from Galveston on a fruit boat across the Gulf to the tiny port of Frontera in Tabasco, inland south and west to Salto de Agua, then on through the jungle to our new home. In a month of travel we left behind all that we had known and entered into a different world.

San Leandro, as I gradually became aware, was the principal plantation, or finca, on the Rubber Company's extensive holdings. From the mountainside south of us, Company land stretched out in a great kidney-shaped parcel of some two hundred thousand acres, its long axis pointing east and north, where the trail wound toward Palenque, a day and a half's ride away. In that direction, as also to the north and the northwest, the land gradually fell away through jungled foothills to open grasslands or campos. Out there the Michol flowed west and north from its source near Palenque to the spot where it joined the Tulija. That was near Salto de Agua, our other "neighboring" town, distant a full two days' ride.

Here and there in the arc fanning out before us were

16

other fincas—Santa Ysabel, the Company's auxiliary establishment where they grew henequen for twine-making, a few hours' ride toward Palenque; San Lorenzo, another henequen finca, a half-day toward Salto; Lumija, La Esperanza, and others farther away in the open savannas, where cattle were the chief product. Behind us, to the south, was nothing—nothing but the towering ridge of Don Juan, and beyond that a great jumble of wooded peaks and rugged valleys, inhabited only by free-living Indians, that stretched seventy-five miles or so to the Guatemalan border and beyond.

Here in San Leandro we lived on the edge of civilization. All about us lay jungle, the sky above us and the red earth beneath framed in dense green-ridged hills. Hard by the village to the west flowed the San Leandro River, a brawling stream here near its source; while a small feeder stream in a gully marked the eastern boundary of our settlement. In all directions trails ran off into the woods, for there, in open valleys and clearings among the hills, were scattered the plantings that gave life and purpose to this place—groves of rubber trees set in straight rows, cornfields to supply staple food for man and beast, stands of orange and lemon and cacao and sugar cane to add variety and sweetness to our daily fare. Meat and milk we had from a few cattle and goats and pigs on the place, while wild game—deer and birds and long-nosed tapir—had its place too on our table. The jungle gave us endless wood for fuel, and there was also a coal deposit up on the mountainside, though it was worked only sporadically. That way too was a limekiln, whose product was used in making cement and in the preparation of cornmeal. Mules—three hundred of them— were our chief means of transportation, going in long strings

17

to the nearby towns for rice and kerosene and other supplies, and periodically carrying the cured rubber, the source of our livelihood, all the way to Frontera for shipment to the States. We had horses for riding, and a small menagerie of tamed native creatures—monkeys and kinkajous and parrots and so forth—lived among the village houses.

Yet Father had seen to it that our surroundings did not entirely lack the foundation stones of the culture from which we had come, or all its amenities. Into the jungle he carried all his books, boxes and boxes of them, packed all the way from the Gulf on muleback. He brought also a small telescope, a piano organ for Mother—who had been a church soloist—and a phonograph and stock of records for all of us. Mother brought her beautiful chinaware, the heavy old family silver, the white damask table linen—heirlooms of our New England colonial ancestors, now incongruously stored away in cedar cabinets and chests in a house without real walls or windows, with only screens to keep out the wild forests that grew all around us. With these things as a material base, with Father's slow, quiet ways and Mother's piquant delight in life as examples, Lucia and I began our growing up.

SAN LEANDRO turned out to be an island in a great sea of isolated jungle. Our mountain ridge was more than two hundred miles from any source of news, or for that matter any large store or doctor or school. Mother had decided to teach us that first year, and Father helped her in giving us lessons in history and geography. I was three years behind Lucia, but I struggled along in her wake, exposed at least to her lessons. They enlarged my scope of learning but gave me a hopeless dunce feeling, since I could never keep up. We had daily lessons, of course, but our best instructors were Charlie Ah Fong, the people of the village, the jungle itself, and Father's immense library. Drawn from this treasure house, everything from Greek mythology and *Les Miserables* to Mark Twain took turns at teaching us the history and drama of mankind. Our pattern of learning in this way continued as long as San Leandro was our home.

As for medical matters, Father had some training and experience. He had also a huge *Materia Medica*, with lurid pictures that made us all too conscious of the weaknesses

19

of the flesh. Horrifying livers, eyes leering out of swollen faces, and symptoms of all the ills of the world were spread on its pages. After a few morbid peeks into this forbidden tome, Lucia and I uncharitably decided against medicine in any form and swore we would never be doctors.

My own conflict with the discovery of fallible self took a dread turn when Mother decided that the book was just the right size for me to sit on at the table. I was beside myself with chagrin over having disobeyed and thus laid myself open to the frightening knowledge in the book. Each plateful of food swam with horrid images of what I sat upon, until tears splashed into the potatoes and Father guessed what I had done. With a roar of laughter he retrieved the *Medica*, locked it in his desk, and gave us a lecture on Eve and the Garden of Eden. Though apt, it did little to ensure unswerving obedience in the future.

We fully expected the diseases we had looked upon to be duplicated in the people around us, but there were few times when anyone among the two hundred families was sick. Machete cuts, an occasional hunter's bullet wound, a jaguar clawing or snake bite, and the inevitable malaria were the worst medical problems. The Indians of these hills were a clean, vital people with even, beautiful teeth and strong bodies that worked hard. They had their own remedies for things, a left-over knowledge from the rich culture of Mayan Empire days. Of course it was thoroughly mixed with witchcraft, lotions and potions and superstition, but some of the herbs were valid medicines duplicated in our own prescription pharmacies: quinine, cala guala for hepatic difficulties, astringents, ergot, blood coagulators, and so on. Father never made any attempt to deny anyone his own kind of brew, but tried to discover what medicinal value it might have. He explained all these things to Mother while she sat sewing in the late afternoons, and the specimens he brought in and reports that came back from laboratories in the United States provided our first lessons in botany, chemistry, and the world of mysterious cures that nature provided. Of course the other side of all this—the signs and omens, the neuroses brought on by curses and fear of poison, the "bad wind" that they believed passed over their houses—was a source of constant warfare between Father's medicine and the native way.

Papa paced up and down, rubbing the palm of his hand against his ruddy beard, staring with a fierce gaze at the finca spread out below the casa grande, as if by looks alone he could clear out superstition.

"That girl's got consumption," he said once, "and they want to feed her nothing but the blood of a black-boned chicken." And another time, "That witch doctor's made a hole in Marcelina's boy's head. To let out evil spirits. I thought trepanning went out with the Incas."

But sometimes the "cures" were efficacious and quite funny. Vampire bats were a source of infection on the necks of the cattle. The people of the village simply made a paste of garlic mashed with milkweed sap and smeared it on the shoulders and heads of the cows. It worked, too, and after a while we used the paste on chicken roosts to keep the bats from causing anemia among the hens, a situation that prevailed in all the flocks and cut down egg supplies.

Then there was the chilío. Among other presents that were continually being brought in by the workers were parrots, baby rabbits, baby javalí—wild pig—and of course puppies and kittens. It was the puppy population that finally brought the chilío down upon us.

One day Lucia and I were playing happily with two half-grown dogs when one of them let out a terrified yelp and raced under the divan. After a few minutes he came out, and then the other began barking and backing up. Finally he rushed out, going right through the screen door. Later we found them both foaming at the mouth and twitching in the garden, but in another hour they came to us sheepishly, wagging tails and seeking comfort, asking forgiveness for their temporary insanity.

It was too curious an ailment to be taken lightly. The attacks were repeated with increasing violence, and Papa decided the pups must have a kind of rabies and had better be shot. This decision came after they went completely mad out in the garden. Lucia and I retreated to the top of the sundial, where we sat with our feet drawn up while the wild red-eyed dogs ran in circles, shrieking in short frightened yelps rather than barks. Papa went for his gun just as Bartolo came in the gate.

Bartolo was horrified at the thought of shooting the dogs. "No, Don Guillermo. I can cure them. They only have the chilío and need momo. Of course if you want to kill them it's your affair, but I assure you I can cure them." His squarish Indian face was passive and his voice slow, but he obviously was shocked at the thought of destroying the animals. His concern, of course, was not because he was fond of dogs, but all Indian families cherished a kennelful for hunting. The more dogs a man had, the greater his prestige; so to Bartolo, who knew all about the chilío, kill-ing these two would be wanton destruction of the most grievous order.

There followed a short discussion of the possibility of curing what seemed to be rabies, while we sat unhappily on the sundial and the dogs ran screaming between Papa's feet into the house. One of them came out the back door, rushed around the side of the house, and ran headlong into the garden house, where the rain gauge and telescope were kept. There he fell over in a heap. Bartolo went to him, picked him up, and with his wide, reassuring grin said he would cure him. Unbelieving but interested, we all trouped into the back yard to watch, keeping a good running distance from Bartolo. Then we witnessed a strange ceremony. First Bartolo picked some large, slightly fuzzy, heart-shaped leaves from a bush that grew outside the fence. We smelled and tasted the leaf that he called momo; it was just like root beer. Charlie, nose wrinkling, admitted that the leaf was not poisonous; in fact it was used in cooking meats such as armadillo.

The momo was properly parboiled and mashed up, then the dark green liquid was poured into an empty vinegar bottle supplied by Charlie. With the air of a surgeon preparing to operate on a serious case, Bartolo, fully cognizant of his audience and his role of prestidigitator, rolled up his sleeves, spread his feet apart, and dashed water on the dog's head.

"Can't give him the momo when he is unconscious," he remarked sagely. The dog came around with a few whimpers and sat up sanely enough. But it was obvious by the slight slavering of his mouth that he would go off again at any minute. Quickly, expertly, Bartolo straddled the dog's

23

back, gripped the head in both hands, pried the mouth open with a stick, and said dramatically, *"Now!"*

Charlie grabbed the bottle of momo, thrust its neck into the dog's mouth, well into his throat, and poured. Whereupon the beast promptly went limp and appeared to die. Bartolo stepped back, wiping his hands on some orange leaves he pulled from a tree near him, and we all watched, waiting for the magic sequence of resuscitation. It came. The dog groaned, heaved in great convulsive shudders, opened his eyes and sat up, wagged his tail, and lay down panting and weary. But the red glint was gone from his eyes, and he was apparently quite normal.

"Just another dose of momo for two more days and he is well," pronounced Bartolo with professional pride. Father, still unconvinced that the dog would recover, promptly gave him to Bartolo.

But it was as Bartolo said. The animal was cured, and he lived to be killed by a jaguar in a glorious fight months later.

Meanwhile the other dog had run to the forest, where we could hear him barking for two days. We tried to catch him, but he ran from us, and later he was found dead.

"This is all very well," Papa said, "but we still don't know what causes the chilío." It took some time to solve the mystery. Papa thought it must be a kind of rabies, although only some of the more obvious symptoms were present. The troubled dogs drank water, which was contrary to the common pattern in cases of hydrophobia. During attacks they ran blindly and did not attempt to bite anything or anyone, which also did not fit into the description we had of rabies.

Other dogs in the village were developing chilío and

24

were being cured by momo. It seemed to us like a veritable enchantment until Father traced it to its cause.

"The dogs get chilío from eating tepesquintla," Mariano told him, looking sideways and down. "They also get it from any wild meat a jaguar has killed. And if they eat danta, the tapir, they are sure to get it. But only during the brama, the mating season."

This made it seem even more peculiar. Then we found out that the chilío was a plant that bore berries at a certain time of the year, which was also mating season for the tepesquintla, a large rodent that lived like an otter in and near streams. The wild razorbacks also liked chilío. During the period of fruiting the berries carried a poison that apparently did not affect herbivorous creatures but had a strange influence on the brain and nervous system of the carnivorous animals that ate them. If the meat was cooked it apparently did not affect dogs, and perhaps that was why humans could eat tepesquintla, wild pig, and so on without ill effects. Papa wondered what would happen if a man ate raw meat during that period, but no one volunteered to experiment.

We had been on the plantation about three months when one night the drums began beating far down in the village. It was a rhythm we hadn't heard before, uneven, exciting, and accompanied by the water drum, a huge hollowed log filled with water and sealed with deer hides that hung under the breadfruit tree below Domotilo's house. Domotilo was the jefe, the overseer of the plantation, and he had an education. But his wife Marcelina, the one whose baby had had a hole cut in his head, belonged to the hills. This was clearly a case of intermarriage between opposing cultures,

25

Papa said, and he thought it would surely bring trouble.

And indeed that night of drumming marked the beginning of troubles to come. Marcelina's mother had walked three days down the mountains from Cankuk near the Guatemalan border, and she had brought with her Marcelina's uncle, known in our area as Don Lencho. He was a famous witch doctor, who traveled about wherever his particular services were "needed." Duly presented at the casa grande by Marcelina and her mother, he was a fascinating figure. He came with an old violin, magenta ribbons tied around his wrists and a green ribbon around his forehead. He wore a jacket of deerskin fringed with pieces of snakeskin, he carried a staff with a crown of wild-boar tusks, and he had piercing eyes that crossed frequently. Of course Domotilo would not have permitted him to come to the house, but he was out in the rubber grove with Father.

Don Lencho succeeded in making quite an impression on us and frightening Mother. Waving his staff about, he chanted all sorts of things, clicking the teeth of a little monkey skull in his hands as he talked. We children stood round-eyed until Charlie, called by Mother, came sailing through the house shouting a mixture of Indian, Spanish, and Chinese and waving his favorite weapon, a meat cleaver. Lucia and I were sorry to see Don Lencho go.

That night things grew more lively. The drums started it. After a while Father sent for Domotilo. We had just finished dinner, and Father, a cigar stuck into his beard where I always supposed his mouth was, sat on the porch at a desk he kept there. Mother was playing casino with us and pretending not to be nervous. But we could see that something was up, for the very sound of the drums made us twitch, and once Lucia had winked at me, I knew that

26

she knew anything could happen. So I sat staring at the
cards trying to remember how to play (I was just learning)
when Domotilo came. There was a long conference. We
were beginning to learn Spanish, and I could understand
a little of what was said, though not much. I sensed only
that the old man who had come that day was making magic
out by the breadfruit tree and Domotilo couldn't do anything to stop it. Then came long, piercing screams that set
us back in our chairs staring at each other. Father got up
and went with Domotilo. Mother quickly put on the loudest
record she could find: John Philip Sousa playing "The Stars
and Stripes Forever." Lucia, with an ear for drama, wanted
to listen to the screams. I went and hid my head under a
pillow.

Papa, in a fine rage, rushed into the village, grabbed Don
Lencho by the collar, and dragged him away from the
drums and down to the hut where he made his brews.
There he found out what had happened. All afternoon
Lencho had been giving "medicine" to various people who
claimed to have ailments. Most of them took what he gave
them without any noticeable results, but one man grew
glassy-eyed within the hour, began to scream, and tried to
run. His lips were flecked with foam, and from time to
time he fell writhing on the floor.

Next, Papa went to see the victim's terrified family. They
assured him that the man was evil. The witch doctor's
medicine was a test of the goodness or badness in a man; it
cured and cleansed him, or it brought out the devil. They
all agreed that the man would die in three days. But none
of them connected the symptoms with chilío. Father did.
He examined Don Lencho's collection of herbs and found
the telltale berries. So this was the secret of the once-a-year

"cures of the soul" that Lencho made in all communities he visited.

Papa, looking around at the faces of the people crowded in and around the small hut, knew that he ran a risk of losing control over them if he interfered. Two hundred families in an isolated jungle could be dangerous if their beliefs were tampered with. They were already in a state of hysteria, moaning, swaying, clapping their hands, shuffling their feet. But he also knew that he had to prove Lencho a fake and murderer if he could. Then too it was dangerous to touch the sick man, who had the tremendous strength of the crazed when his attacks came.

Don Lencho had carefully prepared the people for what was to come. Either out of personal and deliberate animosity toward this village man, or for a fee, he had given him the fatal berry juice, picked during the poisonous spring season. The man, supposedly possessed of evil spirits not unmasked until now, would give everyone ample three-day demonstrations of his affiliation with the devil, through his convulsions and terrified screams. His subsequent death would be accepted by all as an inevitable result of the man's own wickedness. No one, not even his family, would mourn him, and the community would be considered "relieved" of his presence.

Papa came stamping into the house in the midst of the storm music from *Wilhelm Tell* turned up as loud as possible. He was grim enough with a desire to send Don Lencho packing. Swearing he would do away with the man, Papa grabbed up his medical kit and went out to his office, a building that stood just outside the west garden. He already had ordered Mariano and Bartolo to get help from whomever would volunteer, bind the victim, and carry him to the office. He realized that he was taking a long chance on having his authority defied, but he believed that the habit of obedience to the manager, whose right to run the place was not questioned, would prevail at least for the moment.

In the office, redolent of demijohns of aguardiente, furnished with a heavy mahogany desk, cabinets of files, surveyor's equipment, and tool chests, they laid the man on the floor. The frightened Bartolo and Mariano turned and fled. If the Patrón wanted dealings with the devil, that was his problem. They would have none of it. Charlie, never daunted by anything, stayed with Papa. Excited, profane in several languages, his queue swinging violently, he rushed back and forth from kitchen to office, shouting at our wide-eyed eager faces staring out from the back porch to "go long, you!"

We could hear screams, thumpings, and moanings, which gradually diminished only to start up again. Corraled by Mother and shooed to the front of the house, we found new excitement. Just beyond the garden gate the villagers had gathered in a silent, tense group. Don Lencho and Marcelina were not there. They had stayed behind to get thoroughly intoxicated on a special drink he had hidden in her house. Without him the mob had no directive, but stood sullenly apprehensive, and for the moment quiet.

Lucia and I were sent to bed, but we stayed wide awake for a long time with elbows propped on the window sill of our bedroom, staring out across the porch through the screen at the people standing in the moonlight beyond the garden gate. The drums were silenced, but once in a while a murmur ran through the crowd like the sound of wind in a tunnel, low, toneless, yet somehow ominous.

29

BY MORNING everything was apparently calm in the village, and the man Carlos was on the way to recovery. In a few days he was quite well, but he was considered marked by all the people in the village and was shunned by everyone, even his own family. It was quite useless to have him stay at San Leandro. Finally Father sent him off to Don Ernesto Rateike's finca, a long day's ride to the east, to see if he could find a place for him in that locality. It was far enough away so that his story would not be known.

In spite of Mother's indignant insistence, Papa did not send Don Lencho away.

"It is a very touchy thing," he explained to her. "You can't just snatch a people's ideas out from under them. This Don Lencho is a tradition, coming from a long line of traditions. I'll have to eradicate him and his ilk little by little. Meanwhile we will control it somehow. Domotilo has beaten Marcelina, and I have put Lencho in a hut with Marcelina's mother and brother down by the pasture, where we can see whenever anyone goes to visit him for cures. Of course the people are none too pleased with me bcause I cured Carlos. They insist it was his destiny to die and I interfered. Well, interference is what they'll get from now on."

Mother was very unhappy about Don Lencho. She had planned to make a formal tour of the village that week, but it was nearly a month before we were permitted to go with her to all the houses, presenting small gifts to the children and looking into the fascinating dark rooms smelling of incense and burning charcoal, where candles in corners lighted strange images, crosses, and always somewhere a picture of Jesus, thorn-crowned.

Our first state visit to the finca village was not at all successful. Dressed in white lawn, with a white lace fichu at her throat and a lace handkerchief delicately scented with violet toilet water, her dark hair piled in a twist and held with a tortoise-shell comb, Mother set forth with parasol and Panama hat to "inspect and visit The People." (We always felt that The People were capitalized when she spoke of them that way, although actually she was always warm and friendly and eager to like them.) We children, in long white stockings, Mary Janes, and white pinafore dresses, were given "suitable" headgear and told to walk behind her. Charlie stood approvingly at the door. He loved anything that savored of punctilio and that kept his lady in her proper position of mistress of all she surveyed. After a bad experience with an Indian wife who ran away with a blue-eyed Mexican, he scorned all heathen, as he, Buddhist that he was, called them. On this our first attempt to sally forth into the village, he stood like a totem in the doorway, for all to see that he regarded the inhabitants of the place with contempt and would keep an eagle eye on everything that took place.

We started well enough. First we stopped at the rubber-curing plant, where workmen were bringing in "milk" fresh from the groves, each man laden with two five-gallon cans on a pole across his shoulders. We held our noses at the sharp smell of the vats where the milk was bubbling in its chemical bath, poked fingers in the round white "planchas" cut from the sheets of rubber that formed on the surface of the cooling vats, and watched the men pressing the last liquid out of the finished product. At this point, with her careful manners and her correct aping of Mother's genuine but controlled interest, Lucia walked about like Meg in *Little Women*. I was wholly captivated by the entire affair, almost fell into the vats, stuck my finger under the press to see if the rubber would give or squash my hand like a clothes-wringer, chattered in higgeldy-piggeldy Spanish to all and sundry, and resolved to return alone to oversee the job of making rubber. We peered into the smokehouse where the curing process was completed, then stepped off the cement ramp and went on our way.

Collecting me with a firm hand, Mother sailed out across the grass compound to the first village house. And there catastrophe met us. The women, who of course had been peering out between the jacuate palings of their houses, came outside to greet her. And so did the little boys. And we saw that, in spite of Mother's admonitions to Papa, he had done nothing about the naked condition of the children. For some reason I could not quite fathom, the little girls always had on a sliplike garment, but the little boys scampered bare and free as an April breeze in and out of the houses. There were some points on which Papa and

32

Mama did not see eye to eye. This was one of them. Papa even admitted a sort of envy for the ease with which little boys ran about uninhibited by trousers, and I too, in long stockings that itched, inwardly rebelled.

Mother stopped in her tracks. In her careful Spanish she asked where the children's clothes were. Consternation. What clothes? Why, clothes—trousers, shirts. Shoes could be foregone, but *clothes!* But, Señora, there were no trousers except for fiestas, and they couldn't be worn every day.

Mother was genuinely shocked. It was not prudishness on her part; it was simply that her world did not allow little girls to walk about among little boys who were not properly covered. Her sense of the fitness of things was outraged, although I am sure she did not condemn these people as a puritan might. She was nevertheless confronted with a situation that was not acceptable and would have to be remedied. We turned about-face and went back to the casa grande, while the village stared. And I am not sure who was more embarrassed, the village women at the obvious distaste La Señora felt for their small boys' condition, or Lucia and I at being the object of all the astonished eyes.

Mother knew what must be done, and she did it. Cloth was sent up from the bodega, the finca store, and for ten days she sewed. Feliciana, the girl who came to the casa to clean, brought measurements and many giggles to the procedure, and she carried back the finished garments to be distributed. Two pairs of trousers for each small boy. To be worn daily.

Papa laughed heartily at the whole thing, but when Mother pouted and tilted her head in a way she had, he kissed the top of her head and said whatever she did was perfect. Then, turning to us, he added, "And don't you girls forget it."

So we accepted the idea of "civilizing" the children. But the village didn't. From then on, whenever we went forth on an inspection or a visit to the finca, naked bodies were snatched hastily from play and thrust into trousers that stayed clean from lack of use. Then the children were sent out again to parade proudly in front of La Señora and Las Niñas.

Mother never won that go-around, but she did think it was funny and laughed about it. "No matter," she said, "so long as they wear their clothes when I go among them."

The question of the women's dress was another sore point. After the newness of our presence at the plantation wore off, some of the ladino wives could be seen whisking across the finca with only their full skirts on, nothing above their fulsome waists. Never having seen a grown person without clothes except in the pictures in a book of great artists that never had impressed me, I was quite taken aback at the grossness of these women. My question as to why they had such "loblollies" brought the rule that they should wear their blouses at all times. Since the Indian women never went uncovered and were considered by the ladino women as mere Indios to be looked down upon, the edict from the casa about blouses was a great triumph for the Tzeltal. Much pleased chattering went on over this in the village, but it did nothing to win Marcelina, who sullenly refused to appear and went off to wash clothes by the river every time one of us came near her house.

Our relationship with the people of the finca always remained distant. From time to time I was allowed to go with Feliciana to spend fascinated hours in the houses, learning to drink sweet corn posole, eating tortillas, and

34

tasting tapir soup. By the hour I watched the people make little clay animals and dolls and figurines for their children and for their altars, or sat beside an old Indian woman while she ground corn on the stone metate, absorbing Spanish and Indian dialects.

I was never allowed more than an hour or two in the village, and never permitted to really play with the children. One small boy of nine, Antonino by name, was appointed my special guardian. He became my companion in forays to the river or the corrals, and rode behind me when I was at last permitted my own horse and went on the morning family rides. We understood each other very well, developed a high sense of companionship, and cherished a loyalty of the sort peculiar to children. Reversing tradition, he played a lanky Sancho Panza to my pudgy Don Quixote. He rescued me from rushing headlong into quicksand; he once plucked me off a barbed-wire fence where I had slipped, gouging my thigh and saturating my clothes and the ground with blood. He stood by and admonished me with quick looks from his long, dark eyes if I forgot to play the lady in front of other children, and rewarded me with shy gifts of fruit or flowers when I succeeded in speaking with proper hauteur and in correct Spanish to the families whose homes I visited.

How Mother happened to relax her vigilance toward my relationship with the village I do not know, but Papa probably had something to do with it. He always seemed aware of what was happening with Lucia and me, although most of his days were spent away from the casa grande. Often he passed the entire day in the saddle, overseeing the work among the rubber trees, inspecting the outlying areas of the widespread finca, going on matters of business to Salto or Palenque or some other town, or exploring the surrounding hill country. Occasionally one of these trips kept him away overnight or even for several days together. We children knew in a dim way that he sometimes met important people, government officials and political leaders, on these excursions. But the few details that we were able to glean, the chance-dropped names of Díaz or Madero, held no significance for us.

Of course I was too small to go on any of these longer trips. But more and more often, as time went on, I rode out with Papa to the rubber groves or to the dark, mysterious mountain and the coal desposits and limekiln.

Lucia, who was not very strong, stayed with Mother at the casa except for our daily morning rides. She spent most of her time with her nose in a book, gleaning drama and derring-do from histories and novels. I heard these stories from her each night after the candle was blown out. The Plantagenets, the Crusades, Genghis Khan, Jupiter, and the Roman Caesars jumbled happily in my mind to the drowsy cicada hum and throb of soft-throated creatures of the jungle night. More than once I had to be pinched awake when the tale went beyond my understanding. I couldn't have been too satisfactory an audience for Lucia's Arabian Nights interpretation of history. Once I set her off in high dudgeon when she demanded, "Did you hear me? Now what story was I telling?"—and sleepily I answered something like, "Lencho and the forty thieves."

So we lived quietly on our remote finca, and mostly to ourselves. Once every three weeks the mail came in, and twice a year we went out on trips to other plantations or towns. Sometimes the long finger of government, the impersonal Thing from the faraway capital, sent a man down through the provinces to check taxes and perform certain other rituals of officialdom. Of course there were visitors on occasion—neighboring finca owners and managers, a man up from Salto to buy chocolate or cattle, an infrequent Rubber Company official or buyer from New York or California. There were some other Americans too, the Robinsons and the Milays, but they were two days' horseback ride away on plantations in the low foothills of our cordilleras.

Outsiders came through the jungle to our gate like mariners through a strange green sea. They gave us something new to talk about for several days and then were gone again, out of our lives for months to come. Señor Pimiento was among these, six feet tall, with the dash and flourish of a grandee; and Mr. Jubert, who acted out everything that had happened to him, jumping up from the table to demonstrate with wild gestures.

Once a government inspector of rubber came in from New York. He was short and fat and very white of skin. Every time the mule he was riding stopped short at a stream, he went over the animal's head into the water. Father, in a tongue-in-cheek mood, had thoroughly indoctrinated our visitor on the sure-footedness of mules the night before, knowing this creature's tendency to balk. But he had to admit the man's pluck when he kept climbing back on and stuck out the whole day in the woods. He stayed only the one day, but a truce was reached before he departed downriver in a cayuco. The inspector admitted he was a greenhorn who had thought he knew everything about plantations and jungles, and Papa owned he had deliberately tried to help him leave early. New York left Chiapas with a good handshake and a laugh all around.

As it happened, Lucia's cloak-and-dagger approach to life soon began to coincide with an uncomfortable reality. History was already changing the world outside. In the dark back rooms of cantinas in Tabasco and Veracruz, inside shuttered houses, revolution was fomenting and the name of Francisco Madero was whispered. Weapons were smuggled in, and plans were made that swept over the country like a grass fire. Into the hinterlands of Chiapas came bands of guerillas, to prepare the way for the overthrow of Díaz and foreign power. For a time, however, none of this came to us directly. Our first hint of trouble began with a German named Henich, who had taken over San Lorenzo finca, the hemequen plantation half a day's ride down the Michol toward Salto.

Mr. Henich (we never gave him the honorary title of Don, and for that matter I do not remember ever having heard his first name) came to San Lorenzo in the first year we were at San Leandro. He was a large, heavy, red-faced man in his thirties, who wore polished military boots, cropped his hair close in German army style, and carried a swagger stick and a brusque manner. His pale round blue eyes stared arrogantly at everyone. His laugh was a solid sort of mirthless roar that struck at one rather than giving pleasure.

Henich first came to visit in a pleasant enough mood. But Mother disliked him from the start, and we girls soon thoroughly hated him, for he kicked our puppies and wrung the neck of Lucia's miniature parrot because it nipped him when he teased it.

It wasn't long before Papa began getting reports from Bartolo and Domotilo that San Lorenzo and Henich were making trouble. The German planter had begun to collect a rough group of workmen, mainly drifters who came to his place from Tabasco. Altogether they were a murderous collection, bringing in guns and ammunition to store on San Lorenzo. They came through Salto, passed other fincas on the Michol, and headed for San Lorenzo. Outwardly they seemed innocent enough. Families came with them, a good cover for a "simple man, poor, looking for work." But they were an uneasy lot, and Father soon began to speak of the men at finca San Lorenzo as the "Henich gang."

With increased unrest in the north, men of this caliber began coming to San Leandro from time to time, but Papa tried to weed them out and to send on their way any whose stories didn't sound right—and any who carried guns. He had made a ruling that no one on our place was to carry arms, but he kept a store of rifles, which were given out to men who wanted to go hunting. His own revolvers were hidden in his desks, one in the office and one in the house.

Aside from our regular two hundred families, workmen came to us from the outside from time to time. They were

for the most part those set adrift from their moorings somewhere else. Hidden as we were in mountains, with dense,
almost untracked jungle between us and the outside, it was
the escaped and the adventurer, the lost and the strayed,
who came through our finca gate looking for work.

All the workmen in Mexico were theoretically free, but
the majority of them nevertheless lived in a state of abject
peonage. With only a few exceptions, Mexican, German,
and American planters alike took merciless advantage of
them. All fincas had stores where the local families bought
supplies on credit secured by future wages. Since most of
the plantations were several days' ride to any village or
town, the bodega was important; it provided the people
with needed sugar, cloth, kerosene, and so on. And buying
on credit was easy. But working off the debt was a different
story; and as long as a man owed money to his patrón, his
"freedom" was only a meaningless technicality, for by law
he could not leave his finca. Since the people were almost
wholly illiterate, the situation was made to order for un-
scrupulous exploitation. The planter could pad the bills to
his heart's content, and the workers would never know it.
Papa told us with anger and disgust of Arauay finca, where
the owner regularly added the date and the year to the
purchases of each family, raising their debt to a sum they
could never repay.

"Small wonder there is unrest and hate among the people," Papa fumed one day. "Look at this family."

We looked. A little knot of people huddled miserably in
front of Father's office. The man had welts across his face,
and his back was still bleeding from lash wounds. The old
woman who squatted beside a sick child had fierce eyes
that blazed rebellion when Papa said he could do nothing

40

to help them. A woman who stood beside her, with three small children and a baby in her arms, cried quietly into her rebozo.

"At least we can feed them," Mother stated firmly, and she sent for Charlie.

But Charlie refused. "Meshlican no good notting!" he said vehemently, attributing to all Mexicans the fickle, wanton character of his runaway wife. "Send to own kind." And he stalked back to the kitchen, his queue hanging down stiffly as it always did when he was affronted.

So Sabatán was sent off to the village to get someone to provide a meal and posole for the family while Father figured out what to do. These were not the first people who had come to us this way. They had managed to leave the plantation of their servitude in the night, hurrying along dark trails, stumbling in mud, and drenched by torrential tropic rains.

Sometimes, as in this case, Father could not do much to help. An order had come from the jefe político of the district in faraway Salto that any families that ran away from San Lorenzo, Henich's finca, were to be returned at once for debt. The order of the jefe político could not be treated with indifference. The family could not stay. But that didn't mean they had to return to Henich's. An hour later they were started on their way up the mountain trail. They would go up past the limekiln, on the secretive, winding, closed path that led through the high jungle and over the mountain toward Tumbalá, a free village of Chol Indians. A man from San Leandro went with them. He was a Chol, with family in Tumbalá. They might not find a way to live in the rocky mountain country, but at least they were on their way.

41

Of course information about this sort of thing got back to Henich. A stiff note requesting that we cease interfering with justice came from San Lorenzo, and Papa said the beans were certainly spilled. Domotilo used a stronger term. "Ya cayó el tigre," he said. "The tiger has fallen; the war is on."

"There are probably few men more relentless when crossed than an ex-German army officer," Father opined ruefully. But he kept right on smuggling out families who came to him in distress, sometimes beaten, sometimes sick, but always frightened.

Our best friend in the vicinity was Don Ernesto Rateike. He visited us at San Leandro most often of all. A German-American, he was in charge of the Rubber Company's Santa Ysabel finca and a cattle rancher on his own. His place, San Juan, was just beyond Palenque town, where he also owned a small store. He had run away from Germany when he was in his teens to avoid compulsory military training under the Kaiser. He had joined relatives near Chicago, and later, following a wanderlust, he had simply drifted off down the world and stayed in this undiscovered spot, where eventually he married and set about raising a family. His whole story, of course, we never knew.

Sometimes Don Ernesto came with his violin tucked under one arm. We liked to sing while he played for us, and sometimes Mother sat at the organ and sang too. He was a young man in his twenties, with very blue eyes, a shock of black hair, an aquiline nose in a rather pointed face, and a gay laugh. He was one of the few men Papa could talk openly with about politics and people.

Father and Don Ernesto rigged up a telephone line between the three fincas and used it for emergencies. There were plenty of them. More often than not, a call would come in the midst of early coffee and Papa would rush off posthaste to square away some trouble. For gradually waves of the revolt that was sweeping over Mexico to the north came to the edge of our jungled hills and brought with them a threat to our serene living. In our second year at the plantation they were incidents only, but they kept us aware and alert. Those who had worn a revolver occasionally now began to carry one all the time. Even the Indians began appearing with a strange and wonderful assortment of carbines and rifles that filtered through to them from the fighting areas. Those who couldn't flourish a handsome revolver could at least sport a fine-looking holster. The dandies wore tooled-leather or jaguar-skin holsters, hanging low, the butt just level with the hand, for a quicker draw. At first Father carried his weapon hidden, but as conditions changed he finally wore it openly. And it was a good thing, as he and Don Ernesto learned.

The telephone line proved to be more danger than assistance. Of course a storm occasionally struck down a tree and broke the line, but there were days when Father came back from mending the wire with a puzzled look on his face. A falling tree does not make a clean knife cut on a telephone wire. So he and Don Ernesto got their heads together and figured out that the trouble was coming from the old source of conflict, Henich.

There was no open quarrel with Henich. On the contrary, he came to the finca often, sitting sprawled on our veranda in Father's best chair, smoking and sipping at the fine brandy Father always served. His porcine frame bulged over the edges of his chair and his hard blue eyes stared insolently at Mother.

43

Apart from finca relations, Mother had her own private warfare with Henich. The moment he rode in, she retired and pretended illness until he left. Father thought the hostess should stay while guests were present, no matter how unwelcome they might be. But after Henich made a snide remark to Mother about some dolls we had left on the divan sans clothes, Papa agreed that she need not appear when he came.

Invariably when the telephone went dead and Father left with his men to meet Don Ernesto and repair the damage, Henich appeared from the west gate, riding in innocently enough, blandly pleasant, to find Mother quite well and about.

These surprise visits became a pattern, and late one afternoon when Henich walked in without the usual courtesy of waiting at the gate for the houseboy, Mother flared at him that he was unwelcome when Father was not at home. Then she went into her room and shut the door. She sent orders to Charlie that he was not to serve dinner, and that Lucia and I were to stay in our room. Henich sat down on the porch angrily, with the air of a man who had come to stay. In an hour a storm blew up from the lowlands and poured sheets of water from a black sky. Lightning serrated the heavens, thunder shuddered the casa, and we knew Father would not ride in before morning. He had probably "holed up," as he called it, at Santa Ysabel for the night. Even if Henich had intended to leave, he couldn't now, and presently he went to the buffet and poured himself a brandy. After he had emptied half the carafe, he began pacing up and down the veranda in front of Mother's door. Lucia and I opened our room door a crack and watched expectantly.

44

Every stamp of Henich's boots rattled his spurs and shook the glasses on the table. Even the organ gave faint tinkles and squeaks. He began muttering, then shouting, in German and English how insulted he was, how the woman had no refinement, how she had no taste. Then he went back and took another drink. Lucia and I couldn't understand a third of what he said, but his rage was unmistakable. "Maybe he will burn down the house," Lucia whispered—half hopefully, I thought.

The rain came down steadily, the devil frogs boomed in the water tanks, and Henich stamped back and forth. Just what he intended to do wasn't clear, but when Charlie came to light the lamps he watched Henich for a few minutes and then slipped out. He came around to our bedroom window in the back, scratched on the screen, and whispered encouragement to us.

"Ho, I fix 'em!" He nodded and winked, a wink that for that time was more potent than Lucia's. Charlie could be formidable. His long Mongolian face masked a staunch and conniving mind. He understood restraint, for he was excellently Oriental, but he also understood the finer side of violence. Only a few nights before he had convinced us of his warrior nature. A possum was in the chicken house. Recklessly indifferent to the fates of the chickens, Charlie fired a volley of shots into the roosts, then dragged the possum out by the tail, emptied a pistol into the animal, and finally beat it to pulp with a club, whooping revenge. We didn't know what Charlie would do about Henich, but we knew it would be no weak measure.

He proved himself equal to the situation. His restraint was superb. Armed literally to the teeth, he simply went and sat in front of Mother's door. His treasured rifle leaned against the wall, the revolver borrowed from Papa's office desk he held in one hand, leaving the other free for emergencies. A large formidable machete lay across his knees, and in his teeth was his favorite carving knife, sharpened to a razor's edge. He said nothing, but simply sat, dozing and nodding, his eyes half-closed, clenching the knife in his teeth and holding the revolver at ease against the machete.

Henich paid no attention to him. He was working himself into a frenzy and obviously did not consider a Chinese cook of any importance at all. If anything, the affrontery of the weapons Charlie presented only served to make him scornful, and except for a kick in his direction when Charlie sat down, he paid no more attention to him.

Henich's voice was becoming thick with abuse and brandy and we girls hungry and sleepy when Charlie began to move. Henich had come closer and closer to Mother's door, even reaching over Charlie's head to thump on it once. Charlie's eyes flew open, and when Henich came past again he moved one foot out quickly. Henich stumbled, but to our disappointment he did not fall. Each time he came by, out shot Charlie's long leg and the German stumbled; but in his muddled state Henich apparently did not connect his trouble with the calm figure that serenely sat cross-legged in front of La Señora's door. Finally, sodden and unwary at last, he fell flat over Charlie's legs and did not get up. Whereupon Charlie calmly rose, sat down upon Henich's prone form, put down the weapons, and folded his arms.

As soon as Charlie had taken over the situation, Mother came out the back door of her room, Lucia and I tiptoed out ours, and Sabatán brought us dinner. We sat at the far end of the long dining table, with the waterproof curtains closed against the wind and rain. Mother's parrot perched on the back of her chair commenting in a conversational tone on the goings on and asking for his share of a rice fritter.

It would be practically impossible to save face for a man found lying on the floor of another man's house with the Chinese cook sitting on top of him. But Father achieved it after a fashion. He and Don Ernesto Rateike rode in together, and between them they got Henich to his feet, poured black coffee into him, and sent him off on his horse.

It is probable that Henich did not quite remember all that happened, but in any case it was several months before he appeared at the finca again. Meantime, the telephone wire was cut at intervals and San Leandro men began to be sniped at from the bush.

I<small>N THE MORNING</small> a child wakes, as he did yesterday, unchanged by dreams or sleep, but by nightfall someone has turned a key in a lock, someone has shifted the prism through which childhood looks at the world. This happened to me in the spring of our third year at San Leandro.

Each morning we had a family ritual, the daily horseback ride. Except when it rained or for some reason Papa couldn't go along, Bartolo had the horses at our gate by eight o'clock. I was now permitted to ride without a lead rein and was tremendously proud of my Indian pony, a black stallion named Prieto. He was trained to jump fences, leap over streams, and race after cattle, but he was tame enough, subdued by an overabundance of years.

We rode out in the damp of early morning, our faces brushed by wet jungle leaves, sunlight bright on rushing streams and dancing in gleaming drops that splashed from waterfalls. The peah bird, town crier of the jungle, warned all and sundry of our approach with his shrill cries. I loved to hear his scolding voice and see his shiny black body hurtle through the treetops. There was nothing gentle about the peah; he had a raucous voice and violent manner. But his cries meant that creatures huddled down in the underbrush and ferns would be safe from Bartolo's rifle, for the peah never warns except when large snakes, jaguars, or humans pass.

These were wonderful rides, full of inquisitive forays, poking at old logs that gleamed with green phosphoresence in the dusk of deep jungle ravines, routing out an armadillo, or investigating caves where we found animal bones and sometimes pottery shards left by an ancient people. Mother always found new kinds of seeds, an air plant for our hanging gardens, and flowers—passion flowers, white ginger, or sprays of orchids plucked from the more open places along rivers. By ten in the morning, before the day's heat really set in, we returned to the finca. Lucia and I always raced each other up the wide grassy compound, scattering dogs, chickens, and pigs, with the village children waving joyously as we went by.

One morning we came back early, and in the middle of our gallop up the sloping compound we reined to a quick halt. Startled, we waited until Father and Mother came up with us. From the trail to Tumbalá, which wound into the forest back of Father's office, came a line of men such as we had never seen. Tall, thin, straight, with long black hair blowing about their shoulders like ancient prophets, they wore tunics of white tapa cloth and bracelets of polished stones and amber. They carried bows as high as themselves, and arrows in alligator pouches hung from their shoulders. On their feet were peculiar sandals, platforms of wood with high leather shields at the back to protect their ankles.

49

Slowly we rode closer and dismounted at our gate. As we stood facing each other I saw dark amber skins and oval eyes, shaded by half-lowered lashes, looking back at me with a steady but unfocused gaze, as if they were not really seeing me at all. It was a way the mountain people had of being present physically but remaining withdrawn until they were confident of their reception. Any quick movement of friendliness was considered gross and very bad manners. So we all stood for a minute or two, looking at each other but neither smiling or speaking.

Then slowly they brought forward a shriveled old woman who sat up very straight on a deerskin stretcher. They set her down in front of them, laid bundles wrapped in deerskins and jaguar hides beside her, stepped back, and waited. The oldest man, who had a short, sparse black beard, thrust his face forward, staring at Papa, and struck a spear, handle down, into the soft earth beside the woman. Still no one said anything.

Papa was looking steadily at them as if sizing up what he saw, and I felt Mother's hand pull me closer to her. I craned my neck around to see our people and couldn't believe what I saw. Antonino was running pell-mell down the village to his house. Bartolo and Mariano had led the horses off a little distance and stood with their backs to us. In the finca village not a person was to be seen. The whole place looked as empty as though they had all disappeared from the land in five minutes.

Then the old woman began a high singsong one-sided conversation with Father. She talked on for about five minutes, occasionally shaking her fist (or so it seemed to us), sometimes pointing to the rest of the group. I couldn't

50

understand a word she said, but Papa did. When she stopped he answered her, putting the palm of his hand against his left shoulder and then the back of his fingers to his forehead. Immediately the men in front of us did the same. Then two or three began opening the bundles and spreading beautiful things out on them. There were woven mats and children's shoes with platform soles of pomoi wood, as light as balsa, with soft deerskin bands; there were alligator pouches and gray glazed pottery decorated in red and black. Mother forgot her fear of the people in her pleasure at the things they had brought, and delightedly she chose two of the pottery pieces. When she chinked them together accidentally, they sounded like fine china.

But it was the people themselves that held me. I stood rooted where I was, looking and looking. Something in their faces, the way they moved, and their low liquid language made me hold my breath. It was as if I had always known there were people like this, and I wanted to shout at them, "I know you, I know you." They looked back at me in a kind of stillness, their eyes clear now, not far away.

The old woman did not want money for the pottery. She wanted to exchange it for salt. They would bring goods like this every month if we would give them permission to cut blocks of salt from the lick up the mountain. Papa explained this to Mother, and an agreement was made. They gathered the bundles together, made the gesture of hand to shoulder and forehead, and turned to go. Then suddenly one of them turned back. With a swift, graceful swing of his body he stooped down in front of me and held up a little pair of the deerskin shoes, pressed them into my hand, and went back to the others. In that moment

51

he had looked directly into my eyes, and I was filled with an almost unbearable excitement as though some secret thing had passed between us.

When they left, walking with the swift strides peculiar to all mountain people, knees slightly bent, bodies erect, the way a panther moves, we all stood looking after them in wonder.

Papa finally said, "These are the Karivís. Not the Caribs, who are head-hunters, but the Karivís. I am glad you have seen them." And I understood that he knew about them and had been with them before on some of his trips into the hills.

When we got into the house I looked at the tiny shoes they had given me. They were much too small for my feet. Hanging by a leather thong to one of the straps was a small square of jade. It was marked simply, with lines that ran from the center to the four corners. It was deep green, soft, and cool to touch.

The ollas Mother bought from the Karivís stood on the bookcases to remind me from time to time of their visit, but the shoes I put away in the back of my drawer, wanting to hide them. Somehow I didn't want to ask Papa about the Karivís, did not want to talk about them. Their presence had done a strange thing to me, and I had to harbor it inside myself, and think about it, and keep the sense of wonder that talking about them might have dispelled.

But Lucia left nothing alone if her curiosity was once aroused. She asked Papa why the people ran when the Karivís came, and he answered simply, "Because they are superstitious." That wasn't enough for Lucia, so one day when Feliciana was cleaning, she asked her about them. Calculating her words to startle the maid into revealing whatever secret the Karivís might have, Lucia stopped her in mid-dusting with the blunt question, "Why do you run away from the Karivís?"

Feliciana literally froze where she stood. "Don't ask about them. They are bad people," she said in a low voice.

"But they are rather nice. They gave us things. They make pottery. None of you make pottery like that. I don't think they are bad at all."

Feliciana was young, perhaps eighteen, with a pretty oval face and long braids with ribbons wound in them. She almost trembled as she tried to stop Lucia from asking any more.

"Don't ever talk of them. You must never even mention their name. They are witches, and make a magic that sometimes brings a bad wind over your house. They never can be followed in the forests because they can put their feet on backward, and the footprints always come toward you. Even when they have gone ahead and you follow, when you catch up with them they are walking toward you, never away. If I dared, I would break both those ollas and bury the pieces."

Her rapid Spanish was whispered in a voice so low we could hardly hear her, and the words tumbled out of her mouth in a kind of frightened jumble. So we didn't know much more than we had before. The mystery was thoroughly relished by Lucia, but it only bewildered me.

Once, after several weeks, I ventured to ask Charlie about the Karivís. Charlie and I had an unfailing afternoon ritual, and from it had developed a kind of secret understanding. After the siesta hours from one to three, when the blaze of sun was topping the west side of the breadfruit tree, he came out of the kitchen and stood on a little stoop by the door, with a large mat tray of rice which he shook and blew to clean it of chaff. That was the signal for me to go out and wait patiently until he felt ready to lift me up on the table just inside the door and share a time of talking and stories. The table was a thick slab of mahogany, polished by daily scraping and scrubbing to a deep red, its surface as smooth as polished stone. It was a good place to sit swinging my legs and watching Charlie's cheeks puff out to blow the chaff into the wind, and the slow smile that came when he turned his eyes to squint down at me. He always wore black silk suits, and they were never dirty. Lucia and I decided that he must have trunks of them.

The kitchen itself was a sanctuary, not to be intruded upon except by invitation. Mother went out once a day only, and we children were roared at and routed if we came while he was cooking. The big black old-fashioned wood stove always steamed with provocative brews that smelled deliciously, and near the door stood sacks of rice and corn and beans, into which Charlie scooped with a gourd, measuring out daily portions with an accurate eye. His meat-chopping block was a source of awe to me, for he always kept two or three finely sharpened knives and at least two cleavers hanging beside it, with one cleaver stuck into the side for handy grabbing. He was nothing loath to snatch it up and wave it at any intruder, and poor Sabatán often came flying out of the kitchen in haste with Charlie and the cleaver close behind, Chinese and Charlie's brand of Spanish spouting out of him. "Anda balunda," he roared on these occasions, his voice sounding like a promise of doom, and no one dared to disobey that multilingual command to get out. Even Lucia and I, who had a right of

54

sorts to give orders, shuddered under the doorsills, as it were, waiting for the storm to pass before we dared set foot in the back yard.

Charlie had come to San Leandro by accident. He had been an importer on his way to New York. Crossing the Gulf in a bad storm, his ship was crippled and finally towed into a Mexican port. He shrugged, said it was his fate, and gave up the life he had known. His world had been completely changed by a storm and by an American law. The law, prohibiting Orientals from entering the United States through Mexico, made it impossible for him to continue his trip, and since his capital was in his chests of goods, most of which were lost, he had no money to return to China. So Charlie Ah Fong stayed on in Mexico and in time became our friend and protector. What his real name was we never knew, or if there was more to the story than he had told us. He wrote long letters in Chinese, read Spanish and English, but never quite learned to speak either of them properly. That he had been an importer we did not doubt, for his rooms, separate from the main house, were full of carved images, teak and ebony chests, and pieces of carved furniture.

Only once or twice did Charlie and I come to logger-heads. Our main problem arose over the way he killed chickens. He hung them by their feet, punctured their throats, and let them bleed, catching the blood in a pan underneath. I was outraged by this, believing they suffered, and we had a real set-to. I ended it by rushing weeping into the house to beg Mother to put a stop to this method of slaughter. But the same unswerving stubbornness that made Charlie impervious to Mother's admonitions about not putting eggs into baking powder biscuits made him impervious also to her suggestion that he chop off the chickens' heads. He simply could not believe that was an acceptable procedure. Chinese had always killed chickens that way, he said. Wringing their necks made them die of suffocation and changed the flavor of the meat; chopping off their heads spilled all the blood, which was useful. Finally, to silence me, he called me one day when we were to have chicken, got a block and his cleaver, and proceeded to sever the head of a rooster. But he hacked at it, hitting carelessly, whacking it a little from side to side, until his point was won. Since he couldn't bring himself to give one firm chop, it was better to leave the matter as it stood. After that I was icily told to go away whenever he was preparing chicken.

Only twice did I ever go into Charlie's quarters behind the kitchen. My first venture made me understand why his wife might well have gone off with almost anyone to get away. Charlie's room was a sanctum sanctorum of dim light, musky odor, incense, silks and satins heavily embroidered, Chinese gods, and heat. By his bed he kept a Bible in Spanish, and a Chinese prayer scroll was under his pillow. When Mother, who had given him the Bible at his request, asked him why he kept both Buddha and Christ in the same room, he answered, "I bow to all possibilities."

Usually Charlie waxed delightedly loquacious about anything I asked. He talked of his childhood in China, of his sisters and brothers, of Confucius and Buddha, and filled me with Chinese fairy tales and legends. But when I asked him about the Karivís, he gave me one of his long, squinting looks. He sucked in his breath and then went back to shaking the tray of rice without answering. I knew better than to push him. In his own time, having thought over my

56

question from all possible angles, he finally spoke, staring out across the yard.

"No good, Cotolina, no good. Leave Karivís alone." And that was that. They were never mentioned between us again. But it did not allay the mystery of the mountain people or my eagerness to see them once more.

LIKE A PRISM, the different facets of plantation life cast lights upon us to color each day. Despite the chore of regular lessons, we children lived with our various interests in a sort of delighted enchantment in which anything seemed possible. When times were dull we took matters into our own hands and peopled the days with figures from history, doctored to our special tastes. Lucia saturated herself with historical information, and I followed behind. We had Saint Joan and Richard Coeur de Lion instead of Dick Tracy. Father's bookcase made excellent castles for our paper-doll lords and ladies. The books became rooms, council chambers, and so on. We used the shelves for corridors, serviced by pawns from Father's chess set as pages, castles and knights as guards. With fine disregard for time horizons, we paged Charlemagne and Charles the Bold of Burgundy from the tome called *The Spiritual World* to a small, repressed-looking copy of *What Every Boy Should Know*.

We had a guillotine too, a macabre affair made of a matchbox with a pair of scissors stuck through it from below and a proper aperture for receiving the heads. The

58

ladies, however, were troublesome. They wore the conical veiled headdresses of medieval times, and we always had to shove and stuff them down into the place prepared. Somehow such crudities as throwing people to lions were of no interest to us. Occasionally we had to behead a special lord or lady because we ran out of other excitement, and as often we pasted the head back on, declared the whole thing a mistake, and restored the villain or villainess to our fold, the better to make mischief among our more stodgy characters. Mother's solid silver tea and coffee service provided beautiful funeral urns.

One day some very weary and very elegant gentlemen from a British rubber company rode in. Mother, in her white handkerchief-linen dress, her hair caught up with a comb of tortoise shell and gold, sat at the serving table to pour tea. The atmosphere was cordially formal and we children sat properly apart, our manners calm but our eyes large with the anticipation of catastrophe. For as we could have told anyone, the tea would not pour.

Concerned investigation uncovered a whole population of beheaded lords steeping inside the pot and blocking the spout. Sabatán's attempts to cleanse it had not included a very complete application of anything but water, and there lay our poor paper heroes, weltering in the guests' tea! My sorrow, I am afraid, was more for the destruction of our historical progeny than for the confusion in the tea service. I don't remember if the guests were amused, but after a thirty-mile horseback ride in the heat, I presume they were not. Mother did what she could to restore confidence in our hospitality, but it was a little difficult to explain the presence of headless Louis XIV in the sugar bowl.

Some of our magnificent renditions of history required

weddings. According to my sister, who was older and knew about such matters, weddings had rice. The ones I knew about had drums and flutes, and a long train of people with masses of flowers, and a bride with a bit of jade at her throat and amber in her hair. But Lucia said rice, and that meant trouble. I must add that she never ran from me in the troubles she inveigled me into. It was an understood code between us, for when anything really difficult came along she stood by. Mine was to act, hers to command in these early years, and my palpitating heart learned a sort of fearlessness in carrying out her orders.

Rice-getting took more than ordinary courage. Charlie's anger was so fierce when we went near his domain unasked that I always suspected him of some kind of strange sacrificial goings-on. Once I found him lying on his bed surrounded by clouds of blue smoke from a long-stemmed pipe. He said nothing and I tiptoed away, guiltily suspecting he knew I had seen and would hold it a mark against me that I had snooped. It made the getting of rice all the more hazardous. Quite sure that I would be annihilated, I stole out to the kitchen at Lucia's command, reached both hands into the rice bag, clutched what I could, and beat a hasty retreat. I think Charlie always knew when I first approached on these occasions, for at the exact second that my fists were filled with rice, a frightful yell burst from his room and he rushed out, Chinese pouring from him like steam from a kettle. He brandished the meat cleaver and bore down on me with what I was sure was murderous intent. I ran so fast I couldn't make any headway, but bobbed up and down in one spot, the spilled rice trailing behind me.

I hardly dared approach the kitchen for days afterward.

Each time I ventured near with uneasy step and beseeching look, the whole place rumbled with Chinese, shaking my soul to its depths and sending me sorrowfully away. But the powers of Caesar, Genghis Khan, and Henry VIII were stronger than my respect for the kitchen and its guardian, and in due time I stole back for more rice to bedeck a bridal procession.

In the life around us, as in our play, melodrama was ever present, sometimes funny, sometimes tragic. My first love must have begun somewhere in my fifth year, and it terminated suddenly a season or two later.

Don Rubén Aguilar came often to our finca. He was about twenty-seven, educated, charming, and very Latin. The youngest son of an aristocratic family, he was in Chiapas waiting for an "unpleasantness" to blow over. I thought him tall and handsome, and he possessed a beautiful spirited horse, a silver-inlaid saddle with wide reins that jangled with dozens of silver coins, and even more important, a particular smile for me. When I saw Don Rubén ride into the finca, his horse prancing nobly up to the garden gate, I kicked my poor Prieto to get him to prance in like manner and dash along beside him. I suffered a twinge of jealousy too, because Lucia was photographed beside Don Rubén and he played casino with her in the dining room after dinner when I was sent to bed. However, like so many ill-timed hero-worshiping loves, mine came to a sorry, unromantic end.

Don Rubén rode into the finca one day lying across his saddle, face down, blood streaming from his thigh and pouring out upon the ground. There was a great running of everyone to help. He was lifted off his horse and carried

61

half-conscious into the house. I rushed to the hammock nearest his door to sit still and listen with horror to the exclamations as his wound was washed and dressed. With the Henich gang prowling through the woods and sometimes shooting at a man instead of a wild turkey, we felt that anything was a possibility. Only the week before there had been a disagreeable encounter, a fist fight in which one man was pushed into the river, where he drowned. Pointedly, it was always a man who had helped with the revolution or who had escaped from some lowland finca who was the victim. And now Don Rubén, our friend!

But in the midst of Father's imprecations and Don Rubén's groans there came a roar of laughter, and even the wounded man began to guffaw.

"Don't," he pleaded. "Don't make me laugh, it's too painful!"

"You idiot. So it wasn't Henich after all. What possessed you! You don't deserve any sympathy." And Father went off into whoops of delight. Sabatán came out, holding a bowl of water, smirking with his head ducked so as not to show he wanted to laugh too. I was horrified. How could they all act like this over a wounded man! I fled to Charlie, who was busy with fixing dinner.

"Charlie, they're laughing at him!"

"Ho, they're not laughing that way, Cotolina. He just shot his own behind because he forget safety catch on revolver. What you think, hah? Seat are very painful place to have bullet put."

Sic transit gloria.

In our skirmishes with Henich it was useless to send for armed help. The shooting was always done by snipers, the

62

cut in the wire left no specific proof as to who did the cutting. In the jungles no one sends for sheriff or police. You catch your man by different methods.

One day Father, Bartolo, and Mariano went out to mend another break in the wire. There had been a storm the night before, and Papa was sure that this time the telephone trouble was due to the wind, not to Henich. So, as he sometimes did, he let me go along. It was always wonderful to be permitted to go with Father anywhere, and I had learned to obey explicitly so that nothing would keep me from these coveted invitations. In the jungle children did not disobey often. One false move when the order to be still had been given might mean a fatal snake bite. A quick order to get on your horse or to run could mean anything from a jaguar to a falling tree, and it was to be obeyed instantly. The whys came afterward. There was an old saying, "Trust your parents and live; don't trust them and no one will cry if you are lost."

The break in the telephone wire turned out to be a good three hours' ride away from the finca, near the place where the trail to Palenque crossed the Michol. To Father's surprise, the line had been cut.

"Not even storms stop this gang," he exclaimed, examining the fallen wires. At the same moment a shot rang out and a bullet grazed the top of Papa's shoulder. I was standing on the far side of Prieto, and thrust my head under his neck to see what was happening. Bartolo and Mariano ducked behind trees, and Papa turned to face the man who had shot at him.

"Come down out of that tree," he yelled, angry clear to his heels, as he put it.

The "man" was a scraggly, gangling boy of about seventeen, who slithered down readily enough and stood shame-faced, his rifle hanging from his hand.

"Well, you simpleton. Next time you shoot at a man, do a better job. If I were dead I couldn't complain against you. Now the best thing is to give you a good thrashing."

"But I didn't want to kill you, Don Guillermo. You saved my brother two years ago," the boy stammered, his eyes wild.

"Then why on earth did you shoot? Hiding in trees shooting at people—it's a disgrace, that's what it is! I know you, you are from San Lorenzo!"

But before Father could grab him by the scruff of the neck, as he intended, another shot thudded into the trunk in front of him. A San Lorenzo man hiding behind a tree had been jumped on by Bartolo, and in the scramble a bullet went wild, barely missing Papa. Grappling for the pistol, they rolled together on the ground, and in a moment Bartolo and the man disappeared over the riverbank. Papa ran to help. It was a prime chance for the boy to shoot again, in the back, but he didn't. He just tossed his rifle into the bushes and ran too, in the opposite direction. Meanwhile Bartolo had the other man down in the water and was holding him under. Papa pulled them both up out of the mud, disarmed the man, and sent him off.

"Tell your master that we are getting tired of this," he yelled after him, "and get off our property and stay off!"

Bartolo, somewhat shaken, wanted to get back to the finca, but Papa said he had come to fix the telephone line, and fix it they would. Mariano reappeared sheepishly, and the mending went on. When it was through, we all went down to the water's edge to drink posole.

Posole is ground cooked corn paste, carried in a ball

64

wrapped in leaves of the toh plant, green and smooth and clean. It is mixed with water in a gourd bowl and taken with brown sugar or chocolate. There are varying opinions as to the tastiness of this drink to the beginner, but to jungle folk it is food and drink and tranquilizer all in one. It is a potent supply of energy, and two-day-old posole, rather moldy and acid with slight fermentation, drunk with white sugar and tangy, sets one back on his heels with the pure knowledge of what the mede of Valhalla was like.

We made the posole slowly, squatting on the sand to scoop water from the swift dark river, mixing the corn paste and sugar in silence, each with his own gourdful. Then we drank, shaking the gourds in circular motion to keep the corn chankins from settling too much at the bottom. No one says anything while drinking posole. It is a time of deep draughts, slow breathing, and relaxation. The Indians believe that only the most perverted killer would dare touch a man at the moment of taking posole.

Finally we washed the gourds, threw the toh leaves out on the water to float downstream so there would always be green toh leaves and posole, and stood up. Father looked at the telephone line over his head.

"It's hardly worth the bother," he said. "For two cents I'd take the whole thing down." But we knew he wouldn't. Thirty miles of telephone wire had been strung through the jungle mountains at too great a cost of time and trouble, and in case of danger it was our only link with a friend who could come and help.

Two weeks later a group of sullen men carrying revolvers and carbines rode into the finca. They said they were policemen, and they demanded Bartolo. The charges? He had willfully attacked a respectable traveler on the trail from

65

San Lorenzo to Palenque. Father was away at the time, and Domotilo, acting as manager, had to let Bartolo go. He was taken off, his hands tied behind him.

Of course Father set about retrieving Bartolo from the hands of the law. He had to make a trip to Salto and to Tuxtla to do it, so the business did not move rapidly. Bartolo in the meantime did not suffer. He had an expansive three weeks in the jail at Salto, drinking heartily with all his friends, roaring with delight into the night as he reiterated the story with full embellishments. He even managed to get the jailer drunk, but being a "man of honor" he simply put the turnkey to sleep in his own bunk and stood guard until the officer was sober. It meant, of course, that for several hours Bartolo was unofficial jailer and had the pleasure of locking up various and sundry who were sent over by the town judge.

If it hadn't been for a small riot one night, Bartolo might still be in the Salto jail. To celebrate the fact that his patrón was in town to bail him out, he bought aguardiente for everyone, and ended by showing that he was a man of parts by tearing the place to pieces. The town judge was delighted to give Father the papers for Bartolo and tell him to take the fellow back to San Leandro, "for pity's sake."

Bartolo returned home, grinning broadly. Father had proved that he could protect his men. There were firing squads for lesser offenses than Bartolo's "crime," but he had never worried. The shooting wall at Tuxtla would not be for him. His patrón was a "man of importance"; he would be protected.

I first found out that father was helping the revolution against Díaz while I was still very small. We made a

66

trip out to Salto that year, and it was there, in Korean Kim's store, that I made the discovery. Since Salto de Agua was flooded by the Tulija River every year or so, the big mercantile house had a large upper story where goods could be stored. It was big and airy, with windows, and one day we went up the stairs to look at some supplies Father needed. There I found a ladder going up into a mysterious half-lighted space above. All ladders are a peculiar kind of invitation, like railroad tracks or a stile and lane. I climbed up without thinking. I was crawling along on hands and knees in musty dark aisles of boxes, sacks of onions, and coils of rope when I came suddenly upon a man. Rounding a pile of heaped-up saddle leather, I bumped into him lying in the dark. I would have fallen face forward if he had not put out his hand. I was so astonished to find a man up there, in this musty place, that I sat staring. In that second of fright he took quick advantage of my silence to say "Hush" and press his finger to his lips.

"I know you," he whispered. "You are Catarina." His voice and smile were gentle, but his eyes were large and dark and had a fierce, almost violent command in them. "Now I am glad you came, for you can keep a secret. You are the daughter of Don Guillermo. He is my friend, and I need to tell him something."

"I'll tell him."

"No, not that way. Here, I'll make a little message."

He took some straw, pulling it off of a packing for bottles of aguardiente that stood beside us, and began weaving it carefully. At first it looked like a doll, but when he turned it sidewise I could see the "M" he had made of its arms and body. In the back he stuck a pin that had a button on it. The button was big and flat and had the picture of a man's face.

"Be careful," he whispered. "Give this to your papa when no one is looking. Don't even say you saw me or that I made you the doll. Play with it, but keep it in your hands so no one sees the pin, and give it to him when you are alone. Now go, and God bless you, for He surely sent you here to me."

My father plucked me off the ladder halfway down. Kim shook his head. "There might be scorpions up there, or anything. Don't go again." He shook his finger at me and looked scared, and Papa took me back to the hotel. I didn't have a chance to say anything or show Papa the doll because there were always people around, but I slipped it into his pocket without his being aware of it. How was I to know that his surprised exclamation when he pulled it out almost gave the whole thing away? A straw doll was insignificant, but with that button on, it meant something else again.

When he came to kiss me good night in the upstairs room at the hotel, I asked him if he had found the doll. We seemed safe and alone inside the white mosquito netting, and I whispered it into his ear before saying my prayers. I could feel the surprise in his shoulders, where my hands were. "You put that in my pocket?"

"Yes."

"Catarina, where is he?"

"Upstairs in Kim's store."

Those were dark days, when the revolution was already sweeping up from the south to join forces with the burning hatreds and fears of the people from the north, who were moving on the capital and Díaz. In Salto Mother

68

was afraid, the people were sullen, and smoldering terror could be seen in the eyes that watched from dark doorways. Sometimes during our stay there we heard the rush of feet and the sudden thud of bodies in the streets at night.

I saw Francisco Madero once again when he went away. He was not a man to forget. He smiled at me, standing there beside the river boat downstream from Salto. He took my father's hand and said, "Help them. Help them all you can, the people have so few to speak for them." And then he left.

His passing by showed me one small thread in the great pattern that involved all of us who lived with these people, though of course I did not understand then all it meant. The only way my father could help, or perhaps I should say the only way he would, was to harbor those who fled from persecution on other fincas. This he always did, and I understood when more and more they came to us, bellies pinched with hunger and backs raw from the lash. But the misery of their bodies could not equal the hopeless sorrow in their faces. They were escaping from those terrors of virtual slavery that only students of Mexico's history can fully understand or even believe.

All too often, when we left San Leandro's safe plateau and forests and ventured into the lowlands, we saw men dragged along the roads behind horses, pulled through the dust or mud by ropes about their arms or sometimes about their necks. We learned to ride by saying nothing, but it was terrible to realize that we could not interfere in any helpful way.

"You can't fight a whole revolution singlehanded," Papa warned us. "Both sides are at fault. Hatred is ugly, whether it is revolutionistas or federalistas who are in power. We'll do what we can for those God sends our way. The rest we cannot help. Some day it will all be over."

So we could only lean with the storm that brewed among the people, and give refuge. Thus far the fighting had not reached us directly. San Leandro stayed aloof on its high plateau. The sun and rain and clean wind blew down its long, straight finca, and we lived at peace with the mountains and ourselves.

A SEVENTH BIRTHDAY is important for understanding many things. You know what you know then, and see quite clearly what you may never see again. You step over a line when you are seven, and afterward nothing happens quite as it did before. Perhaps it is then that you first know you are you, and God is God, and the earth is the earth. Perhaps those children who never are allowed to stand by themselves and listen have no chance to know that seven begins something new. Perhaps without an attic or an apple or ceiba tree to shelter hours alone, children never make that first discovery of being.

In these Chiapas hills there is something more than birthday cake and mañanitas on the day you complete your seventh year. Everyone comes to you with something new in his eyes. This day you begin your eighth year—and start a new dimension. All the previous year you make discoveries, and then one day the year is done and you are seven. Sometimes significance is what man makes it. Sometimes it makes itself, and then man crosses himself or bows to Mecca or lights torches across the hills, and things that had no meaning take on importance.

Such a significance came to me on the night of my seventh birthday. There were blue torches burning high on Don Juan, and everyone knew it was the Karivís holding rituals in the hills. Like signals the blue flares moved in the night, and there were always seven.

"Look, Papa, the Karivís know that I am seven!"

We were sitting out in the garden looking through his telescope at the Southern Cross. He was doing some paper or other about the top star and was telling me about it.

"It's of the first magnitude," he said, and he told me how he knew. I could only stare at its brilliance, an orb of light hanging in the deep, fathomless space between me and infinity. But my mind was on the blue torchlights.

"There are seven and so am I."

"It is the same thing—the lights, the magnitude of a star, and being seven," he answered.

In a little while I went to sleep, leaning against his knee while he worked, a blanket tucked around me against the mountain chill. I did not dream of the star but of the people who walked the high hills, closer to the star then we, carrying torches that burned blue in the night.

At this time twenty-six plantationers defied the murmur of danger that rumbled in the towns and rode together to the Mayan ruins at Palenque. It was quite a pilgrimage —a real cavalcade of ladies in divided skirts, sombreros jangling with silver coins and plain cork helmets, polished boots and handsome mounts. Mother and Father rode out early one morning to join them, and that was the day I went into the jungle, alone.

72

A traveling missionary had been at the finca and had left his solemn admonitions behind in Lucia's willing hands. Turning from the dastardly intrigues of medieval Europe, Lucia suddenly discovered the dramatic possibilities of getting religion. Each morning after breakfast she sat me down and delivered an impromptu sermon. That morning Lucia's homily was about searching for God. When she admonished me to go out into the highways and byways and look for God, I took her literally. Just what highways were not specified, so it was a simple thing to do.

The trail back of Father's office was forbidden and dangerous. In the jungle one did not go alone on forbidden trails, but this time I felt quite righteous in what I was doing and set off without sense of guilt. I ran along, hardly knowing where I ran. I was content to hear the soft plup of my sandals on the ground, to look at and love every bird, every bright leaf in the glistening morning. The papaya grove was a good place too, hung with green and yellow fruit.

Quite suddenly the trail turned into the forest. This was where we rode up through the darkest jungle to the lime-kiln—a place we called black jungle because of its forbidding dank growth. Black jungle had a way of engendering fears even in the least superstitious person, and the legend that gogols and other wild spirits haunted this canyon ordinarily would have stopped me.

But now I wasn't afraid of anything. God surely could not be very far away. Around a bend, and around another. The woods closed in upon the trail. Lianas hung down with their heart-shaped philodendron leaves, and shadows grew into a green darkness. Everything was still wet from

73

the night rain, but it was beautiful to me, and I joyously marked some heliconia spears, red and yellow, pushing up into a small spot of sunlight that drifted down through the trees above.

I knew stories about the limekiln and Don Juan Mountain, and I had heard that there were duendes also, who lived in places such as these woods. I knew that there was a stream ahead where things had happened, and that the people of San Leandro would not go to the limekiln at a certain time of the moon, and never at night. Was this that time of the moon? But it wasn't night. I shook off the first creepy thought of fear. Gogols were nothing to me. Let them be giants with no bones in their bodies that fell on you; today was today, and I was seven and looking for God.

Around another bend, and I stopped running. My walk grew slower and slower, for the jungle here was a formidable thing. It was the first time I had ever been alone in it, and I knew that danger, hidden but real enough, lay on every jungle trail.

A white-pebbled stream crossed in front of me at the foot of the hill near the limekiln. The water ran with a gogol laugh under a log, and deeper places were full of shadows. I knew a colored iguana lived down there, its yellow trail ringed with black. I had seen it once on a morning ride. We had stopped to look at it, with its blue body, jade-green head and crest, and saphire eyes. "They" said that the blue iguana was the last dragon, symbol of the ancient world, and that all wisdom was his. If you could find one and ask him the right question, you would know how the world was made and when it would end.

I peered into the water looking for the iguana. Had

God told him the Secret? But what question did one ask? And how did one ask an iguana anything? There was nothing in the water but some small fish swimming, and each white limestone pebble shone clean and clear. In the deeps under the log I knew I should not look, for if the iguana were there he might do a witchery upon me. Feliciana had told me about it, all the dark fears of generations hiding in her eyes. She had said the iguana was more than a thousand centuries old and knew all the secrets of Xabalba, the place that was neither here nor there, where man bided his time waiting for eternity. She had told me that things long gone could come out and hold a man transfixed with knowledge he should never have, and that he might die there, standing on his own feet. But if he did not die he would come away quite mad, and could never talk with other men again.

All these things seemed quite possible under the dark jungle canopy that morning. Father had laughed at the legend, and yet I could not look for the iguana. I knew, somehow, that God might not be there.

When I lifted my head I became aware of people standing on the other side of the stream. A small group of Karivís had come out of the woods without a sound and was walking down the trail toward me. I do not know how many there were—five, maybe six. They carried spears, arrows, and bows, and they walked easily, lightly.

I stood watching them come across the water, unable to run, filled with something that was fear and an excited exultation at the same time. They stopped in front of me, standing with their feet in the clear running water, holding their sandals, looking up to where I stood on the bank.

The old man moved first, wading across the stream, stopping to put on his sandals, and then coming up to where I stood.

"Ix im," he said, like a question. I did not know how to answer, but could only look up into the hawklike face. For a moment I was lifted, dangled for inspection by black and penetrating eyes. Then gradually they lost their fierceness, and a gentleness came into them. Like a small creature set at peace after a fright, I was engulfed in a tremendous wonder, and stood looking at the strange quiet of their faces that were like terra-cotta images come alive.

His voice did not rumble or come down upon me like thunder, as I somehow expected. It scarcely seemed to have any weight at all, yet it was throaty, like the low notes of an oboe. He asked softly in Spanish, "Where do you go?"

Without thinking, I said the thing I had almost forgotten: "I am looking for God." I did not specify what God, but although he surely had a different one from mine, he seemed to understand.

"Xa," he said, nodding, and amusement crinkled at his eyes. "But look now, you passed Him. Down the trail, a long way back."

"I did not know." And I began to cry a little, not hard, but quietly, from excitement, tears spilling from my eyes.

Instantly they were all stooping about me, jabbering quickly in Mayan among themselves, their voices like the sounds of water in the river rapids. They reached out and felt my dress, my hair, and patted my arm. Their eyes were bright and eager, and they looked anxiously into mine. Only the leader kept standing. After a moment he walked a little away from us and stood looking down

76

the trail. Then finally he turned and said, "Mah," and they sat back on their heels and said nothing, but looked up at him. They sat on their heels with their arms resting on their knees, their hands hanging loosely from their wrists, their faces waiting, expectant; and I felt their expectancy and stopped crying.

"You are looking for God. Do you want to see Him?"

I could not answer. I suppose I nodded, but suddenly I wasn't sure I could really look at God if I found Him.

"You will stand here," he said, "until you know what you will know. Listen carefully; there will be no voice like mine to tell you more. When you know what you will know, in that moment you will go into the forest, slowly, until you know when you are to stop. And then in a little, you will come back to the trail. Nothing more, do you understand?"

I heard what he said, but I did not understand. "You will do this." He repeated the instructions. Then they all stood up and went down the trail around a tree trunk, past the mafafa leaves, and were gone.

I stood all alone in the forest, in the quiet, listening jungle, and the trail seemed to go nowhere, either forward or back; but where it turned, the trees and vines were thick as though there were no way through them. The Karivís had gone, but it was different now. I did not feel alone and was no longer frightened at all.

Far above the jungle mat, the tree crests moved in a morning wind and sunlight shone on high, distant leaves.

Then, my eyes becoming accustomed to the varying depths of forest about me, which I had not really looked at before, I began to see things differently. I saw little delicate flower cascades high above my head, and a trogon,

77

a bird in ocher and fustic, poised on a branch almost within my reach. Along a tree branch, above my head, was a finger-thick green snakeling more than five feet long. Quietly, almost without perceptible movement, the forest around me changed, and grew closer, and watched me with its inquisitive eyes. Sitting in a tree crotch just beyond the trail was a dark howler monkey, with a baby on her back, pushing the twig-leaves away from her face as she peered at me, gazing off into space when she saw me return her look. She stuffed some of the leaves into her mouth, as though she were taking her midday meal and I was of no consequence. She was silky-haired, and her face was serene, not wizened and frightened with the hopeless knowledge of other monkey folk.

I was unafraid, with a still, listening sort of confidence that I had not known before. I knew somewhere in the back of my mind that to get even ten feet off the trail was almost certain to mean disaster, and that I could be hope-lessly lost almost immediately. I knew too about bush-masters and jaguars, but they seemed to be part of the fears of men, and suddenly I did not belong to the world of men any longer. I was alone in something that I had been hungry to find, something I had understood only vaguely when the Karivís looked at me. Slowly I walked up the trail a few feet to a little break in the growth, and slipped through. Immediately I was out of sight of the trail, walking on a heavy mat of leaves and small branches, surrounded by the great living beingness that was the jungle.

I do not know how long I stood so under the trees. There were no mosquitoes so high in the hills at that time of year. There was no stir of air. There was nothing to hurt or frighten me, and yet at first I held my breath in a tremulous awe. I listened, and nothing moved. I slowly turned about and saw a long, mottled shape materialize out of the mottled shadows and drift way into darker shadows. And presently, as I stood, the jungle began to go about its own way again, as though it had taken a deep breath when I intruded into the heart of it, watched for a moment, and then, accepting me, gone on about its own breathing, its own serene living. I felt a tremendous excitement, and a comfort, as one might feel on walking into a room where there had been fearsome sounds, only to find in it the warm calm welcome of a place one had always known.

Perhaps some primordial sense in me responded to the steamy warmth of this cradle of life, this womb out of which had grown from time's own beginning all things that live. Perhaps I had slipped out of the outer sheath of humanness and stood, not entirely myself but a girl-child only, in the warm bath of fecundity that was the core of the jungle. Perhaps that was what the Karivís meant to have happen when they sent their own children alone into jungle to listen, and to be.

Nothing more happened. It did not need to. I was surrounded by something that was not movement or sound or color but a silent, intense awareness.

Presently I looked down. At my feet, newly fallen on the deep humus, lay a large tacalate seed, the red-brown bean from the tacalate vine that carried clean water in its great winding stem. The seed was as big as the palm of my hand, and I held it there, gently touching its smooth, shiny surface with my fingers, discovering for the first time the meaning of a dark brown seed. For a moment I thought

79

I would take it with me, a talisman. And then I knew not to, and laid it carefully back on the moist ground.

After that I went back to the trail, slipping through the break in the jungle as easily as I had come. It was no trouble for me to know the way back. I simply returned, but how I could not have said. How you return like that I still cannot tell anyone, for once inside jungle it all looks the same, and each tree is just like the last one passed.

The trail was empty as I went back, but I knew the Karivís were not far from me. They had their own ways of going.

At the papaya grove San Leandro spread out before me, open in the morning sun. A woman crossed far down the village, her bright embroidered blouse a slash of color against the green.

I went and sat in the shade by the breadfruit tree. Charlie was castigating some recalcitrant in the back yard, and somewhere far off the spider monkeys set up a chattering. Lucia came to look for me, anxious and doubtful. She stood under the tree a long time staring at me before she asked, "Did you look for God?"

But I could not answer, for there was nothing I could say.

THE KARIVÍS camped outside the finca across the San Leandro River, where a milpa, a corn field, had just been cleared. The smoke from their supper fires made a thin spiral of blue beyond the river trees. The air was still, waiting for the rain, and the smoke hung in streamers across the canyon.

I knew I did not dare go alone, so I bullied Bartolo into going too.

"Idiot," I called him when he objected. "Idiot, I'll go alone then." He knew I probably wouldn't, but it served to give him an excuse if we were caught.

So we went off to the river, down the clean path, with Bartolo scolding and muttering all the way. We crossed on a fallen log that had orchids dangling from the moist branches, and went through a patch of black woods. The Karivís were camped at the edge of the clearing, near a giant ceiba tree. It was a tree I loved, for it stood sentinel at the beginning of dark mahogany woods. I could see it from the house veranda, its straight white bole towering high above the other trees, its branches hung with oriole

81

nests that swung in the wind like long Christmas stock-ings. It was beautiful even in the rain, when drifting mists passed over its branches and made a phantom of its spreading crest. And now the Karivís were sitting at its feet, and I could go and sit there too.

They had made temporary shelters, one-sided thatches that slanted upward from the ground, their backs to the wind. Over one fire some meat was roasting, hanging on a tripod. Over another a great black pot steamed and boiled. Two women were cutting big cubes of white salt into small pieces. Another woman strung a pile of peppers, red and green.

The men sat on their heels, their elbows resting on their knees, their hands hanging idle. They were talking to-gether, their voices a murmur like the sound of water falling at a distance. How can anyone describe the Mayan speech? It is full of throaty stops and liquid *l's* and rush-ing *sh's*. It is a language unlike any other, but belonging to the incorporate language of all Amerind peoples.

I stopped hesitant at the edge of the milpa. In the quickly passing dusk there was an enchantment in the low fires, in the bas-relief of the strange faces, Their talk was a murmur only, a movement in the quiet. Far off, the perdiz gave its longing, flutelike call.

Bartolo made his last plea. He filled my ears with im-precations against them; they were witches, it was danger-ous, we must go back. His round Chamula face was puck-ered with anxiety. He even threatened to leave me there. I looked at him and shrugged.

"I am not afraid. You are a man, what is the matter with you?"

82

Bartolo sat down on a log and said nothing. I knew he would wait for me, and I walked slowly into the clearing. Everyone stopped talking, stopped moving. All eyes were turned toward me; a head lifted, a hand dropped, and a silence full of question fell about me.

The old man I had seen on the trail sat under the tree near a fire. He stood up and waited for me to come. We looked at each other for a few moments. He was smiling, his eyes warm and alive. They were strange eyes, that could look so full of a glow like charcoal embers and still could be remote, as if impenetrable curtains had been drawn across his awareness.

Slowly he leaned down and made the gesture of acceptance that I was to learn so well: the back of his fingers to his forehead and to mine, then the heel of his hand brought hard against his left shoulder—a reverse of the gesture he had used with Father.

"Max—ich-im," he said. I could not answer because I didn't know how to speak their tongue, so I stood and looked back, smiling too. I was here, with a breathless sort of excitement, unafraid, and all their strangeness was not strange at all, but something I seemed to know about, something I wanted to be with. I was happy, loving their faces that were so different from all the other faces I had ever known, their long, graceful hands, the flowing ease with which they moved.

There was a flat white stone on one side of the fire, and when the old man pointed to it, I sat down. The others turned back to their own fires and began to talk again in low voices, as if nothing had happened. I might have been a leaf fallen from a tree settled into its place at the ceiba.

Then all the questions I had about them came to my thinking and so to my lips, and I began in Spanish, "Where do you come from?"

The man, who said his name was Caiya Uum, the leader, the wayfinder, took a small stick of cedar heavy with resin and lighted it at the fire.

"This fire," he said, "is as old as any man who has ever lived in all these hills. It was begun thousands of years before our time and has never gone out. We bring it with us in little copal ollas, like this." He lifted up a small pot of baked red clay, with a face on it and a wrist and hand for a handle. "We are never without this fire. It is the only thing we have left alive out of all Mayapán, except ourselves."

I did not understand, so he explained, holding the sliver of cedar while he talked, looking at the glowing point of it, not at me.

"We are the Maya. We came from the east, we came out of the morning to the beginning of a new place. We lighted a new fire, we began. Hunab Ku, the All-God, was the only one who knew. He saw, and sent Itzamná his son to earth to teach man how to use his right hand, how to make the corn and cacao and myriad good things of the earth come into being, how to build out of stone the monuments to the Great Belief. Itzamná was made into child and then man, with a right hand that blessed, and in turn the earth blessed him. Palenque is his city. There he walked among the people and watched them grow. Copán is his last place. There lies his hand, buried beneath a monument; there lies the torch of all man's knowing, sent from Hunab Ku, the All-God.

"We are the Maya. We grew, built, believed from the

84

first day of our empire, tun ahau, the beginning. And when came the day of transition, the day of changes, we asked no questions but sealed our cities against the day of returning and went away. We traveled in the darkness of long years, hungry sometimes, lost. We came to shores, and these shores rested us. They gave us salt and food. We built again. Again rose cities of stone, and we called it Mayapán, the kingdom of the Itza.

"But here Itzamná did not come. There was only the memory, and the memory grew thin among the people. The day came when man killed man, who had never killed before. From the east more landed on the shore, this time not in pilgrimage but to rob and burn and kill. The mothers hung from trees, the children from their own mothers' feet. It was a time of darkness when our pride betrayed us.

"When all this came to be, we left our cities once again, wandering, hidden, keeping our sacred fire, not forgetting Itzamná. Our life is a pilgrimage, waiting out the time until we build once more. To the north cities will fall, man will kill man and brother destroy his own birthright.

"Itzamná has not forgotten us. The promise that was buried with his hand, the torch, will live. We will build cities of stone once more, build them upon the bodies and the promises of those who walk with Hunab Ku, and there will be beauty and laughter on earth, and sorrow we will not, not again.

"Here and now we live in this place of Xíbalba. It is neither here nor there; this is the place where man must find himself, and find himself by forgetting all he imagines himself to be. For here Cimi, protector of lost things, guards all our souls, and here we dream and wait and bide our time, keeping the sacred things sacred, waiting."

85

When he finished, a low chanting began all around us, the sound weaving in and out as one sang and then another. A high falsetto carried the long, keening notes, and response came from around the fires.

Rain came slanting over the mountains, and shadows reached across the milpa. The woods loomed dark, forbiddingly, in front of us, and I heard the big conch shell at the casa grande blowing all home for the night. Bartolo waited at the edge of the small woods, and I stood up to go.

No one moved. Caiya Uum sat back, his hands limp in his lap, palms up. He stared at the earth and did not raise his head, but sat in a remoteness, unreachable, lost in a thinking beyond us all.

So I went back—across the milpa, into the trees, over the log bridge at the river, and up to the house, where a white cloth lay on the table and Charlie was lighting the lamp for supper.

From the veranda I could see the ceiba tree and the drifting smoke of Karíví fires. Then the silver sheen of early rain came over the finca and the sudden tropic night closed around us. Down in the village a bonfire glowed wetly in the dark.

The people of the finca village did not welcome the coming of the Karivís, whom they thought to be witches and regarded with superstitious dread. They never went near the encampment at the ceiba tree, never spoke to us of the casa grande concerning these people of the mountains. But we learned that Don Lencho spent several days making incantations against them; and when this did not

86

result in their moving on, he packed his own belongings, monkey skull and all, and departed from the village—never to return, it was said.

Unconcerned about all this and hardly even aware of it, I spent the next days with the Karivís. There was no trouble at the big house about where I was. I always took Bartolo with me, and since it was usual for me to be at the corral, or watching the saddle-maker, or down at the stream wading, few questions were asked. It was useless to take Antonino along. He simply turned and ran every time I mentioned the Karivís.

In these days Lucia was submerged in books and did not take her nose out of them except to instruct or exhort me when I appeared. I lost interest in all the usual pastimes. The thirty-five parrots that preened their feathers in their veranda corner went undisturbed, and except for the usual visit with Charlie after noon dinner, to watch him blow chaff from his tray of rice and listen to his stories of China, I stayed with the Karivís all day.

They greeted me in the same way each day, and whatever he was doing, Caiya Uum stopped to sit with me. Na Ná (grandmother in Mayan) sat with us when we talked, watching intently, instructing me through Caiya Uum. She was little and very old. Her eyes were deep, alive with a tremendous force. Her hands were the claws of a bird, her face furrowed parchment. But her body was straight and she moved with grace and ease. She came each day to touch my arm and look down into my face. Then the lessons began, for lessons they were.

"Now you are here and we can talk together," Caiya Uum said, "it is time for you to learn these things." Each day I wondered, "Why are they excited when I come? Why do they want to teach me these things? What are they trying to say to me?" But I could never ask them these questions. I was drawn to them with excitement and expectation too, and I could not have said why.

They taught me all the names of the ancient citadels: Pusil-Há, near water, where the best pottery was made; Xíbalba, now called Palenque, where the bodies of the great Mayans lay, where the true treasure of Maya was hidden; Palenque, the city of lost souls, the sacred city, for it was Itzamná's own. Copán, Uxmal, Tikal, Yaxchilán —all these names they taught me and where they were. For some they had their own names, and they told me of places the world has not yet heard of: Xabán, Xuipá, Chi Huí, Chi Vol, and the most beautiful, Y'aix-Há.

It was when they were teaching me to count that we came to our first astonished difference.

"This," said Caiya Uum, drawing a symbol in the ground with his cedar stick, "this is the zero, the whole."

"But zero is nothing. You begin with *one!*"

"No, zero is *all*. Zero begins!"

Caiya Uum gazed at me in bewilderment. He said something rapidly to the others, and they looked their consternation. I was lost. I felt as if I had said a terrible thing, but I couldn't understand what could be bad about zero being nothing. That was what zero meant, wasn't it?

In silence we looked at each other. He had drawn into himself, and his face had a look of remoteness. Na Ná's face was a mask, her eyes looking out across the group of people. They were sorting peppers, making arrows, or just sitting in the shade making music with strange little

88

clay tlatils. Their music was a haunting sound, a rhythm, a song like someone calling. Full of nostalgia, sometimes with little quick cadences like laughter, it sang and wailed and haunted the ceiba with its melody.

Then Caiya Uum took his cedar stick and put it into the fire and began to speak in a low, quiet voice.

"Zero is the beginning. It is the whole. There is no 'nothing.' It is impossible for anything to be without something, without being. Zero is the whole of everything, the snake with its tail in its mouth, the beginning and the end. To have less is still part of the whole, like half an orange. To have more is creation, the whole added to and yet still the same, simply larger. A whole could be ten miles or a hundred miles, but it would be a unit just the same, a zero. How can anyone think of nothing?" He looked away from the cedar stick burning in his hand, and for a minute his eyes locked with mine in a deep, penetrating gaze. It was a look no one could forget, filled with such strength, such knowing of something powerful and sure, and a kind of glory in the Knowing. And as he looked at me he repeated the question, which was really a statement.

"To think of nothing is to think emptiness, and there is no such unless it be without Hunab Ku. Those people who start with nothing are those who deny their life and being and think themselves the creators."

They showed me the sign for zero, a sign like a cotyledon beginning to sprout, a seed from which all things come.

"And that is where Hunab Ku puts his gift of being, in the zero, the core of all things. We move out from that core in all the myriad ways of life and being, and if one

89

thing is cut down another takes its place. Even an abyss is filled, although it may be filled with things our eyes cannot see."

They taught me that all things moved in rhythm—the sun, the moon, the earth, the seasons, the coming and going of all things. It was a dance, a movement that had its own music, loud or soft, horrible or divine depending on the ear that heard, the interpretation, the listener. They showed me how the stars moved and where and when and how the moon came and went. I knew some of it, and I wanted to show them how Saturn looked through Father's telescope, but they laughed and drew the rings around it when I told them, and named the colors. How they knew I did not know, but they said it was "old wisdom."

I asked them who Itzamná was, and they answered, "I-ixh, the morning star." And I asked who his mother was, and they answered, "The star that rises out of the sea at sundown." But if I pressed them further, their eyes only grew remote and they did not answer.

So I asked them how the earth came to be, and they told me there would be four creations, each in a different dimension. Each would be destroyed, one by drought, one by flood, one by man, and the fourth by fire, when even man would be consumed. And to my question, "And then what happens to people? Will they all die?" they answered that the people would become ashes or light, as Hunab Ku chose.

For all their love of the sky, they did not despise the clay of the earth. They put their hands upon it lovingly, and planted seeds with care in its dark embrace. They buried their dead under their own houses, and left the houses to cover all the days of living that had been in that place. "For to mourn and cry and hold the beloved is to deny his freedom, to keep it forever threaded to our lives. The body goes, and no one should deny the soul its transition."

They told me there were three kinds of sickness, of body, of mind, and of the soul. "And man can die more easily of the last than of any, even though his body stay alive. Each time you forget Hunab Ku you die a little."

But they were not always serious, not always telling me of their history or showing me the secrets of their belief. They joked too, delighted at their own humor, their eyes twinkling, sometimes chortling out loud in glee. They told me the moon was only a piece of tortilla that one of the gods tossed over his shoulder to the poor. And the poor nibbled at it and nibbled at its edges, holding it in their thin little hands until it was gone. And if you looked carefully at it when it was round, you would see where the tortilla was browned by lying on the fire.

"It is the way the gods take care of the poor, and feed their spirits so they can look up with happiness and say, 'The moon is full again!'"

They told me about shooting stars, too, laughing among themselves. "The gods sit talking in the night, gossiping about the ways of men, as they like to do. They sit around their fires and talk and smoke cigars, long ones, from the tobacco of the hills. And when a cigar burns low, they toss the stub away, and it streaks across the sky, and men think it is a star falling and call it a mystery." So I shared, too, their whimsical kind of legendry, and when they told these stories the children came and stood shyly listening, looking at each other with bright luminous eyes.

They had been there five days at the milpa, and with

them I had shared the pasty macal root and the new corn and the deer meat and the popostle, a coffeelike drink made from roasted corn. I sat huddled with them when the rain came, and laughed with them and was silent with them, and finally on the fifth day they were gathering their things together to leave.

"Your mother and father come today," they told me.

"How do you know?"

"We know."

I walked back up the hill from the river that afternoon sad and lonely. I was glad Mother and Father were coming, but with that gladness was a hurt I could not dig out of my mind. Why did the Karivís have to leave? What was happening? Some big change was coming, and although they did not say so, I knew that nothing would be exactly as it had been before. For I was beginning to learn how to know things as they did. So I walked slowly up the slope past the plantain leaves, past the lemon trees, through the green grass to the garden gate. I was thinking, "When will they come again?" But the only answer was the call of a bird that flew up from the pastures crying, "Después, después—later, later" as it flew.

OTHER and Father came home with plans for a trip to the States. We read the joy of anticipation in Mother's face, and we knew how she would welcome this respite from the isolation of her life on the finca and the maraudings of the Henich gang. Her pleasure made us all happy, but a frightened tightness came and sat between my shoulders. Suddenly San Leandro was to be taken from me. Me from it, of course; but I had not asked to go. How long would we be away? How far would we go? When would we be back?

"Three months, just to California. We'll be back by Christmas."

How many miles to Babylon? Threescore miles and ten. Christmas was a thousand years away and California farther than the moon. Earlier, I had not cared when we made trips away from San Leandro. But now the States seemed so far away. It would be three weeks of horseback and boat just to the Gulf, unless we went via Mexico City. That meant a week more by train, climbing up from Veracruz. I remembered Mexico City as a glimmer of

93

lights far down the mountain. It was beautiful from the high pass, but so many long hours winding and twisting down into the valley of Tenochtitlán would be hard to bear, and we would still be two thousand miles from California. By boat it would take days across the Gulf, when sometimes even the parrots we took with us would be seasick. Sometimes the load would shift in a storm, and we would see the horizon of the United States come into being through a weary and nauseated gaze.

I went to bed to hang onto the pillow and lie wide-eyed in the warm dark. The Karivís—when would I see them again? They were my people now. Their words had no harshness, and their hands, even when they held a wild thing, gave it no fright.

I finally fell asleep but awakened suddenly thinking someone had called me. It was all very quiet, and only the cicadas with their constant strumming hum spoke for the things that live in the night. Even the devil frogs in the big tanks were still. I got up and went to the front screen to look out at the sleeping village, and beyond, to the left, at the ceiba tree. The moon was a quarter gone, desolate-looking, tipped to one side; but it was bright enough to illuminate all the houses and make a path of light down the finca. The pergola of the bandstand with its wrought-iron openwork was a dark valentine against the sky.

I opened the door softly, went to the garden gate, and stood there listening. What could I hear? No sound, certainly, for the coming dark of the moon was a silent time when things slept. A warm, faint wind drifted in from the mountain, pushing at me softly. It was not a matter of thinking about what I wanted to do. The path to the river wandered off at right angles from the gate, and my feet took me there. Where I was going and what I might expect were of no concern. There was no deliberation, but as on the day I ventured into the jungle alone, I simply went. I heard the wind, heard the ceiba tree and the quiet rushing river in between; but if it was not a sound aloud that my ears discerned, it was none the less strong.

The grass was wet with the heavy tropic dew, and my feet felt quick and light walking on it. It was a good thing to do, and this going in the night was good. My mind said I would not go as far as the milpa, that I would only walk out a little toward it in the night light. But my feet kept on walking to the stream.

For a moment, there beside the river, I hesitated. There was a patch of dark woods to cross before I could reach the milpa and the ceiba. Jaguars lived all through these thickets, and I was alone. Here was where a jaguar had chased the goats, running after the little gray one that was the last to cross. He had come in broad daylight, and this was night.

Then I heard a sound, muted, as if it were a long distance away. It was an open palm and then fingers on the surface of a long drum. Then it changed subtly; an indecisive tone came into it, an inflection hesitant, uncertain. For a second I wanted to run back up the slope to the garden, but the moon came sliding out from behind the tall black-tipped trees and made a lake of light in the water at my feet.

I crossed the log lightly, forgetting again that jaguars lived in the woods, that coral snakes sometimes lay along the trail. It was dark in the forest. I walked slowly, aware again of the overpowering closeness of things, of eyes that watched, of things that breathed but did not move until I passed. At the edge of the milpa the moonlight was clear

95

and pale. I could see the little glowing fires of the sleeping Karivís. Quickly I walked directly to the ceiba and to Caiya Uum.

He sat leaning back against the tree, his face lifted, looking up toward Don Juan, but something had happened to him. I had never see him like this before. He looked small, withdrawn, diminished, his eyes dark reflections in the sharp mold of his face. At his feet sat a boy of about twelve, who stood up when I came. He wore wide bands of thin gold about his wrists and ankles, his hair fell long and black about his shoulders, and instead of the white tunic the others wore he had only a loincloth that had folds hanging in front, dyed in reds and black.

Caiya Uum did not speak or turn his head. He was gone from that place, and yet there was his body breathing, his presence strong as though he reached out and touched me. The boy looked at me but said nothing. Although we had never see each other before, we touched shoulders with our finger tips as was the custom. I sat down on the white stone near Caiya Uum and turned toward the hills. There, high on the mountain, were blue flares, seven of them, moving slowly on the great blackness that was Don Juan. What did they mean? I turned to Caiya Uum to ask, but he was lost and distant. It was as though he were not a living being but a mummy, given life once more, living in some other sphere, with a shrunken body like a dried seed. Gone completely were the strength and magnificence of his austerity. I could not even see his eyes, to know whether they were tender or sorrowful or angry. They were deep in his face, shadows only. I was afraid—afraid for him, for what seemed to have happened—and I put out my hand and touched his knee.

96

"Caiya Uum. They are taking me away. I am going to have to go away, Caiya Uum."

The boy turned and looked at me and then at the old man. He said something quickly in Mayan, and Caiya Uum sighed and turned to look down at me. His eyes were full of a great quiet, the lids half-down as though he were sleeping still while he woke.

"Caiya Uum, I have to go. Why do I have to go?"

For a moment his smile was an illumination, the whole of his face glorified with it, but his only answer was, "The wind has changed, Catarina."

After a while he began to tell me things; things I was to remember. He leaned down, still remote and diffident, still shrunken and terribly old.

"What is life? It is a moment. It is never the same. It is now, not yesterday or tomorrow. It is this." And he picked up a leaf new-fallen from a branch. "It is this thing." He laid it in the palm of his hand, down low by the fire so the glow would show it clearly.

"Where is life? In this leaf? Will it be there in an hour, tomorrow, in a year? But it is there now. This instant it is living. What you do now is important to living. Not what you will do. Change comes to all things. Go with it, and you live. It is because this leaf cannot change that it must cease to be a leaf. The wind has changed, Catarina; go with it."

He said something in Mayan to the boy, who went and spoke to the sleeping Karivís. They came silently in their white tunics to sit near Caiya Uum's fire, burning small pots of copal, nodding and murmuring among themselves. The boy brought a gourd full of a strange-smelling liquid and handed it to Caiya Uum.

97

"This is the drink of new corn," he said. "This is only from red kernels, never from white. It is the blood of harvest, blessed."

Caiya Uum sipped a little and handed me the gourd. I drank a swallow, but it was strong and sharp-flavored. Then the boy carried the gourd to each Karíví in turn, even to the small cluster of women who stood to one side. They took a swallow each and sat back on their heels in silence, sometimes blowing a little on the pots of copal, sometimes just sitting with their faces turned toward Caiya Uum. They were stone monoliths of an ancient empire, alive and moving and waiting to share something with me alone.

Then Caiya Uum began to talk softly about where I was going, how far away it would be but how near. He said that I would return and we would talk again. But there might be some things I would need to know to help in the days to come.

"Have you seen deer drinking at a stream?"

"Yes."

"You see how they stand in the clear water. First they sip a little, then lift their heads to listen. They sip and listen and sip again, relishing the cool wet against their slim legs, the cool water taste in their mouths. They never gulp or raven at the water. They do not need to. It is the half-starved or the overindulged who cannot wait to carry off food or drink. It is the jaguar too well fed that tears and claws at his food lest he need to share it. For he is unsure; he overfeeds lest no more come, he gluts himself lest he must give up some of his pleasure. It is only the one who is unafraid, whose body is hungry but not his soul, who dares to stand easily, drinking slowly, knowing the taste of each clean drop, knowing that where this came from there will always be more."

Caiya Uum stood up very slowly, and his old power grew in him. He came to my white stone and stooped beside me. "Look. Wherever you go, these three things you must know how to make."

He fashioned a little pyramid of stones and earth and on the smooth place on top put three crosses, symbols of the trinity of man, earth, and god. He put the largest cross in the center of the pyramid.

"The center cross is perfect. That is the spirit, the flame. That must stand free, for it is Hunab Ku, and it never will belong to your body although your body may harbor it. Each smaller cross is your self."

He bent down one arm on each of the smaller crosses and put them on the pyramid, one on each side of the large cross.

"One of these is your intellect, the other is your physical self. They are never sufficient in themselves. They are not perfect. They cannot exist one without the other. These three you must place before you often, so that you will remember who and what you are. These three live in all men, but only one is Hunab Ku."

Caiya Uum went back and sat under the tree. All his vigor and strength and the strange glory of his vital being seemed to drain out of him before my eyes, and he disappeared into a fragile old, old man, sitting slumped under a great tree in the red firelight.

"Caiya Uum, why does this happen to you? Where are you going? What is wrong?"

Caiya Uum shrugged and lifted his face to the mountain,

99

and his voice was so low I could hardly hear him. "The wind has changed," he whispered, and the corners of his mouth lifted as though he were smiling to himself.

We all sat in silence, and the moon went low in the sky. The first calls of the howlers began like great organ notes, echoing up from the canyons where they went to drink. When the Karivís stood up and the fire was only glowing embers, the boy said "Come," and we started together toward the trail.

The boy walked through the woods with me, across the log to the trail that led up to the house. There he stopped, and we touched shoulders lightly with our finger tips.

"My name is Sac Chel. Do not forget us."

I walked up the trail. It was dark now, and cool with the passing night. Sac Chel stood watching until I topped the hill. When I looked back, he was only a deeper shadow in the shadows by the stream.

It was not until years later that I found out that Father knew of my going, that he watched in the garden and was not afraid for me, for he too knew the Karivís.

ON THE DAY of
our leaving, a thin quarter-slice of the darkening moon hung
low in the sky to the west and the morning star was still
brilliant in the pale east when we climbed into our saddles.
As we rode out through the village the people came silently to their doors to watch us go. The dogs did not
bark, and only the flickering of red coals in the houses
we passed spoke of movement and the morning to come.
At the gate we looked back. On the rooftree of the casa
grande a blue heron perched, outlined against the dawn
sky. The blue heron is the albatross of these hills; and
Bartolo nodded and smiled at me, and Antonino pointed.

"The blue heron, Catarina. You will come back."

The jungle was dark, and white mist rose from the canyons where the rivers were. A deer bounded across the
trail, and wild "pheasant," as everyone called the guans
native to these jungles, flew up suddenly with a rush of
wings. We heard the howling monkeys roaring down to
the river to drink, and slowly the forest about us light-
ened. We rode on the winding trail out of the higher

101

mountains to the foothills, to finca Santa Ysabel, breakfast, and the day. At sundown we reached Don Ernesto's
finca San Juan near Palenque, where we planned to stay
a few days.

That night there was much talk of the nearby Mayan
ruins, and finally Papa decided we should all go and see
them before we left. So we rode up the next morning,
Don Ernesto, Mother, Father, Lucia, and I, and stayed the
day, eating lunch under the great amate trees by the pool
called the Queen's Bath. It was my first visit to the pyramids and temples the Karivís had told me about. Few of
the buildings had been cleared at all, but those that stood
free of the forest stared with empty corridors across the
sea of treetops that spread down the mountain. They stood
silently, listening to the forest—for listening they seemed
to be, waiting for a footfall or the touch of the hands that
had made them.

I climbed a tower, and was sure I would never come
down again, for I felt I had quite left the world. I could
see out and out toward Campeche, Tabasco, and the Gulf.
Here in the mysterious corridors and stairways of an
ancient people I was quite alone. I could see Mother
and Lucia walking in the courtyard below. I was separated from them by height and by the crowded trees and
vines below me, and they seemed very far away.

The tower went up three flights; there had been a
fourth, but it had crumbled into rubble that sent down
a small shower of stones when I climbed up and sat on
the top. There I perched, looking and looking out toward
the sea where I must go, then back into the hills, into the
heart of the jungle. Now I was level with the tops of the
towering forest. There hung cascades of flowering vines,

tree ferns, and lianas with their dark green, wide leaves. All the living creatures of the tropical forest were deep in there, hiding, chirping, whispering, and staring at the humans who walked in this ancient citadel that they had taken for their own. The tower was a rock garden of begonias and ferns, delicate pinks and purples against the gray-green lichen and the cobweb gray of the stones. From its turret I could see glimpses of other buildings yet to be discovered, under the spreading foliage of the trees below me, where roots and trunks twisted up through fallen roofs and vines curled around the pillars and bas-reliefs of Itzamná himself. When Papa called me, I came down and took the long way around the outer corridor, just to be alone for a few more minutes. The walls had prayer niches in them, shaped like a T, where Papa said the people put their foreheads and their hands when pray-ing, standing thus in the shape of a tau or Mayan cross. I understood these crosses. They were part of Caiya Uum's teaching.

Just before I turned the last corner of the outer court, I sensed that something had moved ahead of me around the wall; and when I made the turn I saw in front of me, standing in a stucco-lined niche, a bowl such as the Karivís made, filled with burning copal. I stood very still, knowing that only the Karivís or one of their clan could have put it there; for no one lived in these ruins, and no one else could have either the pottery or the copal.

As we rode back to Palenque Don Ernesto talked a good deal about the Karivís, calling them wild people. He said they often came to worship in the ruins but never went near the town, where like as not the people would have driven them away or captured them as savages. I found it hard to hear our friend talking that way about them, and once I looked at Papa. He shook his head and kept his own counsel, and so did I.

All the way to the Gulf—for we were going by boat after all—we felt the pressure and change of the revolution. The oppressed people had turned on the landowners, and now innocent and guilty on both sides were suffering alike. Fincas burned; people moved from place to place, carrying what clothes and possessions they could, as refugees always have and always will run from human hate. We heard stories of the marauding groups that went under the banner of revolucionistas or federalistas, and it was hard to say which were the more brutal, which destroyed the most. In these provinces, especially in Tabasco, there were no real armies, no real war, but a melee of factions fought a constant guerilla warfare. Sometimes it seemed that no one was really fighting for anything, but only using his political affiliation as an excuse to kill and plunder.

On the river boat that took us down the Usumacinta, the people crowded onto the lower deck humbly, bowed under great loads of whatever they could rescue from their ranches or villages. Among them always were soldiers, sometimes recognizable as such only by an officer's cap, or a carbine, or a military coat. They were friendly enough with the people, singing and joking and helping a woman here or swinging a baby up onto a shoulder there. But there was no response from the women and their families. The only men who accompanied the women were the sick and the old, for all the young, even boys, were marching on the land. Women and children stared with lackluster eyes and huddled together near boxes of merchandise piled on the deck.

At Jonuta we went ashore while wood was loaded for fuel. We had a friend there, a rancher who owned wide cattle ranges. When he learned that the boat was to be tied up for two days, he invited us to his estate. To get there we took a motorboat two hours up a tributary of the Usumacinta. It was a beautiful craft, swift and exciting as it pushed across still lagoons and up narrow feeder streams. Its passing sent great waves crashing among the water lilies and hyacinths that grew from bank to bank, tangling them in the propellers and tossing them, fragrant and bruised, from the river into our laps.

The ranch-house partition walls were made entirely of bamboo, with mattings for ceilings under the tile roof. At dinner I looked up to see a face peering down at me. It was covered with reddish brown hair, and it squinted and blinked and ran out its tongue. Señora Montejo, our hostess, laughed at our consternation and called, "Martino, come down."

He was a howler monkey, one of the red variety, a rarity in these lowlands. He was about the size of a four-year-old child, and he went among us with great dignity, giving each his hand solemnly. When he came to me he curled his tail around the leg of my chair and stayed beside me. I gave him a banana, and a friendship was begun. It was a strange friendship, for my loneliness and his discovered a bond in each other, and after dinner I sat with him on the porch, his head in my lap, stroking his neck and ears, talking to him, and pretending he could understand all I said because he was from the forests I knew.

It was still early, for dinner is a midday meal in the

tropics, and we went for a walk in the garden. I suppose no one dreamed that I would go wandering, but the garden was new to me, and it had paths and flower beds and a brick walk. Walking erect, holding my hand, his tail around one of my ankles, Martino accompanied me through a side gate and toward a cluster of trees. As the edge of the grove I saw people moving and heard a great cry go up from many throats, a cry of anguish. What I saw there brought clearly to me, in one awful scene, what a revolution could mean.

A heavy beamed frame stood in the center of the group of wailing men and women. It was the kind of thing made for a hanging. But it was being used for a far more terrible act. An old man, an Indian, and his two sons were hung there by their hips, upside down and naked in the sun. Ropes had been passed between their legs, strapped tight, rubbing and burning the flesh of their loins as they swung. The two younger ones died as I stood there, the old one lived on. I saw him swing himself forward once and catch the rope with his teeth, to hold himself and so ease the pain. He was a strong old man, with muscles like tough fiber, and he held himself half-erect by his teeth until he became unconscious.

Too frightened to cry, I turned and ran back to the house, threw myself down on the steps, and held Martino close to me, rocking back and forth in an agony. This was something about which I could do nothing. It is hard to know like this, before you are ten, how men can suffer, and to know that there is no way to stop it. But a fierce anguish grew in me against the man who owned this ranch, against all power that could make these things possible. Martino seemed to sense my torment and crooned to me as

106

I rocked him, patting my hair and making low, clucking noises in his throat, as softly I began to cry.

Mother could not have known what had happened, so I cannot blame her for her startled order to get away from the monkey when she came out on the porch and saw Martino half-smothering me in his long-armed embrace. Of course she thought he was hurting me because I was crying, and she leaned down to pull me away. Instantly Martino let out a roaring cry, leaped out of my arms, and with one bound was on her shoulders his tail strangling tight around her throat, his hands tearing at her hair.

It was a terrible moment, for I could not make him hear me as I screamed for him to come down. It was only seconds before Papa and Señor Montejo came running to help. Mother had fainted from the fright of it, and Señor Montejo put a chain around Martino and tied him to a tree far enough away from the porch so that he could not reach us. I stood sorrowfully looking at him, and he stared back at me, showing his teeth and emitting short barks of fury. The thing we had shared was broken. He had tried to protect me, and now he was thoroughly bewildered and angry with everyone. Suddenly feeling that everything was wrong and that something valid had been betrayed, I sat down and cried again, this time quite alone.

By the time we reached Frontera and the boat that was to take us to Galveston, Father realized that he could not go with us. The war was technically over, but the whole country was uneasy. We had escaped the actual battles, but now the provinces were full of men and boys who no longer had homes to go back to, who had learned to live off the land by looting and shooting, taking what they

107

wanted and not having to work for it, and in this atmosphere the Henich gang too would be active. San Leandro would be in greater danger than ever.

Papa left us at the boat, saying that in three months if things were safe he would telegraph us to meet him in Frontera again. I knew that with his whole heart he did not want to close the plantation, and would take a long chance rather than leave. Somewhat comforted by his parting kiss and his promise, "Don't worry, Catarina, we will be back together at San Leandro soon," I climbed up the steep gangplank and waved good-by.

Part II

IN ANOTHER AUTUMN, two years later, I stood on the Gulf's edge at Galveston, Texas. Once more we had been in the States, this time for five months; for a trip to California every so often had become a regular pattern for Mother and us children. In the spring we had left a peaceful, prosperous San Leandro, little troubled by the tides of revolution or the spiteful gnat bites of Henich and his gang. We had seen a bit more of the outside world; we had come to know our aunts and uncles somewhat better; we had had our first disconcerting taste of formal schooling. Now we were waiting to go home.

The Gulf stretched blue and green and dark gray under white clouds that piled up, motionless, in the hot autumn sky. I could smell the damp heat that was like home, and I dug my toes into the white sand of the beach with a quick need to hurry across that wide expanse of water. Out there, beyond the farthest seeing, south and south, lay the little town of Frontera, at the mouth of the Usumacinta River. And up that river, twisting and winding and twisting, three hundred miles of it, my father would be getting ready to meet us.

A creature whose instinct tells him he belongs in a certain place on earth is set whimpering in eagerness when he approaches that place, hurting with anxiety to be gathered into its arms. So I leaned into the southern wind and became still with a terrible kind of awareness, as though the place I loved so much could speak aloud and take away the hurt, the sickening ache and need to hurry, that made it hard to breathe, that made the ground beneath my feet feel so strange.

I sat down on the white sand at a place where tiny waves could lap my feet, where shells filled with the sea lay near me and large gulls stood by, one-legged, waiting. Not waiting for anything; just waiting.

I sat and dug my heels into the sand. Birds lazily skimmed over the water, and the whole world stopped. There were only the slowly undulating green-gray Gulf and the birds that passed and wheeled and passed again. There never had been anything else. Out beyond the edge of the world there was no Frontera, there was no San Leandro; there were only the sand, the water, and the birds. And God put His face down close to me and said You are You, and you know how the sand feels between your toes, and how wet the wet is, and how hot the sun. And in this minute there is only this, and it is good.

But the urgency came back after a moment, the sense of haste, as though something were waiting for me while I idled at my childhood. How many miles to Babylon? Three-score miles and ten. Will we be there by candlelight? Aye, and home again.

How far is threescore and ten? And how far is far? The distance of the thickness of a door is far. And sometimes the distance to the moon is near, or even no distance at all. Especially if you stand in the moonlight. No farther than from my forehead to my father when his hand pushed the hair from my temples in a way he had. I made a small pyramid in the sand, wanting to put my three crosses on it, remembering the Karivís. But the sea came up and washed it away, so I lay down and drew the design in the sand.

Some young girls, laughing and squealing, rushed down to the water and rushed away again. Then three young men dove into the warm Gulf and swam to the raft, far out. I turned my head to watch them, and finally turned over to sit up and stare. Why did only the men swim out? Why did the girls just stand and jump over the silly little waves and squeal? Were they afraid? Or had they just forgotten something?

And why was it that Mother sat so primly, with her big hat and her high shoes? Once she must have loved sand and water. What happened that made wonderful full-of-laughter people stop being part of things?

It was sad. I lay there, half in and half out of the water, and held the gleaming sand in my hands and was sad for her. But she wasn't sad. She was laughing. Had she forgotten how to lie like this and let water from far places wash warm and loving on her feet? Or was there some terrible tabu that came into women's lives when they crossed the line into grownuphood and made it impossible to do this? And if they did do it, would they be ridiculous and only try to play, not knowing how any longer? Or would something wonderful happen to them, so that they

113

would know better than to wear high shoes and corsets and tight stiff collars even in the heat? Didn't their feet ache to get into the sand? Not ever?

I would never wear high shoes. Or high collars. And I would never forget how to ache my feet into the sand. And with a sudden new sureness of a nebulous thing I didn't understand at all, I knew that even the hurt about being so far from the jungles was a good hurt, one not to be lost. It was to be borne, even cherished. To yearn like this meant something. I needed to keep on yearning and hurting with the love of it. If I stopped, something would be lost.

I got up, quiet with my thinking, not anxious for the boat any more, and went to sit by my mother, to listen to her woman's talk and the shush of the sea.

When the ship came, we were told she was the *Deica*, a freighter from Sweden, sail and steam. She arrived in Galveston from the Torrid Zone loaded with rotting bananas and pulled into dock, circled by screaming gulls and clouds of gnats. The sailors had scooped the defunct cargo out onto the reeking decks, and we went down to see her, holding our noses, hot in the September sun, picking our way along the oily planks of the waterfront and not altogether happy. Mother's parasol provided a small pool of shade, and her full skirts that swung decorously from side to side gave us a protection of sorts from the strange sailors and beady-eyed traders who openly stared.

Captain Oleson regretfully told us that we would have to board the vessel that night, for she would sail at dawn. The cargo, he admitted, could not be jettisoned until next morning when we were out of harbor, past the three-mile limit.

114

The accommodations were a small cabin on the deck near the stern, which the captain was willing to give us, and a saloon with red plush upholstered chairs and much polished brass. She had two holds and a charthouse. Her two masts pointed to the hot, sultry sky, the black snout of her funnel stuck up stubbily between. On her prow was a figurehead, weatherworn and unholy. I stared at it, while Mother, her skirts held up off the wharf, talked with the captain.

The figurehead that loomed above me was a large half-naked woman carved in wood. Her paint was peeling. One eye stared blankly at nothing; the other was round and frightening, set at a curious angle to her brow. The huge grapes in her hands were a faded red; they were pressed against her naked, peeling bosoms. Her body disappeared somehow into the ship's prow. What was her face lifted to see, and why was she there?

We boarded the *Deica* at sundown. Our wicker trunk and the small heavy one from Paris almost filled the little cabin. Our suitcases were stored on a lower berth. Mother went to bed as soon as it grew dark; her sea misery was already upon her, set off by the reek of the rotting brown mass on deck. Bed was, of course, the other lower bunk in the stuffy cabin. Lucia and I were a bit hardier; we sat out on the cooler afterdeck. Back there near the rail the air moved a little now and then. The night was full of stars and silence, with a few boat lights winking on and off around the bay. We finally fell asleep uncomfortably in our chairs, out feet tucked up under our white nighties to avoid mosquitoes, our faces hidden under a shawl spread across us both.

It was still dark when we awoke with a breath of cool air and the sound of a mighty scraping blowing about our

115

ears. The sailors were clearing the decks, and the *Deica* was slipping out, already miles from the shore line. It was dawn in the east. As the Gulf swells turned from an abyss of dark water-shadow to gray, then deep blue-green, the morning came. The *Deica*, clean once more, turned her nose into the heavy swells, heading south by east. By mid-morning, like a respectable middle-aged matron, she swung hippily out to sea.

There is always a small moment of panic when a ship goes out and the last line of land drifts into the distance, merges with the horizon, and at last disappears. Suddenly you are out in a vastness with nothing to catch hold of. It is the land that has left you; the sea has pushed the earth away and left you adrift in spaciousness, with liquid beneath you and infinity above. I knew that somehow, within a week, the sea would push us to the other side of the Gulf and I would see Frontera coming toward us out of the morning. The throbbing of motors had taken us out of the harbor; now the sails were filling in the wind and carrying us along. But even they didn't seem to have much to do with our going. They were something man fixed up to help the motion of the sea. We had set our faces south, and south we would go until the wind changed. That was what Caiya Uum had said: "The wind has changed." Had it changed again now that we were going home?

Mother lay unhappy in the cabin for most of the voyage, Lucia played casino in the saloon with the captain and the first mate, and I roamed the vessel. Lucia, now past twelve, had moved somehow out of our childhood. I, with only nine years, didn't understand quite what had happened. People treated her differently, and although the

116

change was a subtle one, we were separated by a difference that brought no comfort to either of us. Although I admired her devotedly, for she seemed more than ever a storybook heroine, the few times we tried to play together were quite unsatisfying. There was no hostility between us, but like two animals, one inside a fence and the other outside, we who had been in the same paddock were suddenly lost to each other. She had left her childhood and moved into the mysterous world of adolesence, had become a lotus-eater, while I still fed upon wild ginger.

Lucia sat hours on end in a chair by the rail, reading a book, her braids looped up over her head in a coronet. Sometimes she decorously sat playing cards with the ship's officers, surrounded by red plush and brass. She probably wasn't feeling superior at all, but she was several eons away from me in doing these things, so I turned to the *Deica* herself for companionship.

Forbidden were the holds, the sailors' quarters, and the charthouse. But the rest was mine. The galley was fascinating in a doubtful sort of way. Potato peelings and astonishing oaths frequently came flying out of its door. The cook was a pirate of a man with a bright bandanna tied snugly over his head, and I lived in lusty fear of him. He had a cat that coveted the parrot, but after the loss of the tip of her tail in a skirmish her disposition was affected, so the captain said, and she was a sour beast. She was enemy to all men, as was the cook, and the two often sat together in the doorway of the galley, glaring at all who passed. He was a big man who wore nothing but trousers, and his flabby, fat white paunch, his hairy arms and chest, and his bellowing voice made him as terrible to me as the great beast Beowulf fought. I fully expected him to turn green or purple or any other preposterous thing. I do not remember his face, although he undoubtedly had one, and although he urged the "leetle girl" to come in and see his kitchen I was terrified, and one look at the red bandanna coming along deck sent me scrambling.

Some of the deck hands were Mexicans, but most of them were Swedish like the captain. They became guardians of my safety and told me stories, whether I could understand them or not. With faces that were tanned to a blister, their violent blue eyes intense and round, their hands horny and rough from toil and water, they laughed and joked and sang songs of the seven seas for me as they washed their faded clothes in buckets or mended sail. I could understand only their laughter and whether it was with me or at me, but their eyes were always kindly, and there was no problem between us.

Sanctuary from all things was offered by a high pile of rope coiled in the prow. There I could lie back and look up into the sky past the rigging; or, standing on the tips of my toes, I could see down past the figurehead into deep water. Down there the prow cut through the smooth combers and turned them back like a giant plow turning green glass earth. It was rhythmic and even, the same again and then again.

Beyond us porpoises dove and cavorted, cleaving the sea without a splash, playing around and around the ship through the hot mornings. Portuguese men-of-war solemnly floated by, small galleons on their own secret voyages, bobbing a little with the ship's passage. Squid swayed in the seaweed-green of the undulating water. Clouds made great shadows on the quiet sea, and sometimes a school of fish, moving swiftly, swept past in one dark pattern just

118

below the surface, an underwater shadow that came and went again. Late in the afternoon sun the flying fish were little silver spoons flung upward.

At night the sky was a vastness alive with star sparkle. Those who know the Gulf say it is unlike any other place; it is its own universe, the stars move alone in their orbits around it, and its waters lap against shores that are distant, the shores of other worlds. These nights were hot, and everyone stayed on deck for what coolness there might be. The sea became a dark, moving body, the mother of all things, gently rocking us as she slept, her arms filled with fantastic progeny.

Once the *City of Mexico* passed our bows, going north. The night hung low with clouds, and without the stars we seemed to stand still in space. We moved under sail, silently in the blackness. Talk had drowsed almost to nothing when someone saw a light to starboard and called out. We strung ourselves along the rail and watched her lantern swing in signal, and a long halloo came across the water giving name and destination. Back went our own cry, and the silent sea shushed and washed against the ship while we waited, listening. Her lantern swung again, and a low call from her haunted night. Our captain's voice gave fair passage north, drifting out into the dark where already distance was coming between us. A light winked on and off, and then we couldn't see her any more. She was a phantom in the black night, unseen but for the glow of the lantern and the fantasy of phosphoresence that trailed her sides and cascaded in her wake. From out there a long, low, honing sound blew into the night and space, drifting into the lonely silence behind her. We stood leaning on the rail, listening. Everything was quiet except the sound of water and the low voices of our sailors. We were alone again with the sea and the night, and once more smoke from pipes hung in the warm Gulf air and the rumble of Scandinavian voices told stories. But I sensed that everything was suddenly different. It was the first mate who spoke to me about it, answering my unspoken question. Men moved across the earth, he said, leaving a message for each other when they passed. But it was a message no one could read very clearly. And it made them sad.

So we stood together, the sailors and I, leaning on the rail, listening to the music of the sea and the great emptiness around us, the smallness and yet the bigness that made people the way they were.

Finally I fell asleep in my rope turret and was carried, limp and content, back to the cabin after half the tropic night had passed over our heads.

We woke to wind and morning. Terrible gusts they were, and the ship was rocking in a great expanse of bright sea and sky, with the sun hard and brittle in the early day. Breakfast was an impossibility, with my cocoa sliding along the table and even the dishes that sat in metal holders splashing their contents. The engines throbbed and men shouted and ran about.

Something wild was happening. It blew in my hair, blew against my eyelids, pressed excitement into my hands and feet so that I scrambled into the rigging, which was forbidden me, and climbed high and higher to see the horizon tip and tilt and turn above and then below me as the ship wallowed in glassy caves and surged to tremendous white-crested heights.

I clung to the rope rungs and shouted and sang into the

120

wind. It was a wild and glorious thing to do, delirious and free, and I gave no thought to danger. The lookout in the crow's-nest saw me and clambered down to fetch me up to his high and perilous perch.

There is no place like a ship's crow's-nest, the caramanchel, high above ship and sea, with a storm blowing out of the north. It jolted hard with the impact of each heavy sea, and we caught spray from the raging combers even up there. Our caramanchel was nothing more than a basket high on the mast, and the distance down was forever, the decks hard and glistening below. Together the sailor and I clung to the basket edge and to each other, and together we saw terror come up out of the north. It was a black cloud, like a cobra hood, that lifted itself above the horizon and moved swiftly toward us across the sky. And what does it do to a soul to hang like that between sea and sky while dread leans down from the heavens? For then the world turns saffron, the sea's rolling eye grows glassy, and all the waves smooth down as if flattened by the hot breath of the god of winds, Huri Kan himself. This is the immensity of violence when gods stir the brew.

Hanging on desperately up there was awesome; and so was the descent, the flight deckward, clutching at the sailor's shoulders, his arm around me so hard that there was no space in me for breath, staring at the deck that came up to meet us as his feet sped down the rope ladder. Once down, he tossed me like a kitten into our cabin and slammed the door.

The first splatter of rain was wet on my face, and I scrambled to the top berth where I could open the porthole and lean out.

In the moments before the hurricane struck, the world

held its breath. In that yellowish dark I heard all hands go running. The sea changed color, became slick and scarcely moving. The sky darkened and lowered until it seemed the horizon itself rose and spread and enveloped us in its hot, moist grasp.

There came a little whine of wind in the ropes, another breathless moment, and then we could hear the roar of it far out—the baying of the thousand deafening voices of the storm, whipped by the wind into a frenzy, racing toward us across the sea. Lightning ran over the ship, and great searing fingers of it marked violence in the black sky. Now the wind struck, twisting the ship around and writhing the glassy water up and up, then dropping us down into the black-green cavern under the ledge of a massive translucent roll of water. Swiftly it swept under us and lifted us prow high, the quivering, crouching ship and all the little, little people on her.

A sailor, running past, grabbed the rail to brace himself, and lightning suddenly shot past his head to strike a hawser ten feet away, splintering and snapping the cable into a twisting hot snake that whipped along the deck. A second later the sailor saw me, gave a shout, and pushed me back inside the window, slamming the port shut.

Throughout the day and into the night I knew why the Indians speak with awe of Huri Kan who walks the earth with his great staff, and of the plumed serpent wound around it, its eyes flashing lightning as it looks here and there across the world. And I knew what Huri Kan's great cape looked like, blowing saffron and black from his god-shoulders, hiding mad violence under the soft gray shafts of rain falling out across the sea.

In those hours I looked deep into the heart of the Gulf

itself, deep into the smoothed-out glassy green of the tormented water as we plunged sideways and the wave washed over us; and I looked up into the eye of the storm, gray and black, blinded with lightning and rain. In those hours I learned something of the passion of the things of this earth.

When the storm was done, Captain Oleson had a thing or two to say about my climb to the crow's-nest. With his blue eyes peering down from under bushy white brows, he asked how I was going to live with the world now. I didn't know what he meant, but he did not smile when he added, "These things are too big. Like Pandora, you shouldn't open boxes that belong to the gods. Your heart will burst with what you have seen. There is more than one danger for a little one in the high caramanchel."

Four days later the *Deica* limped into Frontera at the mouth of the Usumacinta River and stuck herself on a sand bar at the entrance of the bay. There we sat, battered and forlorn in the tropic sun, waiting for the little tug to come puffing out from port, for the swarm of officious health officers, aduaneros, collectors, and hangers-on. But beyond the cluster of roofs and the banana groves, the Usumacinta and the jungle waited for me. Already a brilliant purple-blue butterfly drifted on lazy wings over our heads.

123

THE VAST DELTA of the Usumacinta River is a labyrinth of deep channels in the dry season, a great inland sea when it rains. Here live white egrets and blue herons and pink flamingos in blue lagoons surrounded by green-black forests. Along this lower expanse there moves a traffic as slow as the meander itself. Big flat-bottomed river boats with side or stern paddle wheels churn upstream once a week and drift downstream in the following week. In the rainy season banana barges pulled by throbbing tugs move through flooded pastures and woods. When the river is low they are lost to view, only their masts visible above the high grass. When the river is high they rise even with the bank, to anchor in the front yards of fincas along the stream. Except by storms or an occasional cayuco, the mat of water lilies and hyacinths is undisturbed. But when storms tear at the inundated land, the lilies break loose and go floating down to the Gulf, and everyone along the river knows that the rains have come.

That morning when we woke to find ourselves on the sand bar outside Frontera, we leaned on the rail of our

124

listing *Deica* and stared into the hot sunlight. Across the water was the low green forest wall, the jungle that came down toward the sea. There was the tile-roofed town standing on a ridge of land between it and the Gulf. In the bay water lapping around us, hyacinths from the upper reaches floated past, nodding gently to us as they drifted by. And we knew the rains had come. We had been delayed in Galveston too long.

The tug that came for us was filled with a motley of mustached officials. The stevedores who swarmed over the rail from rowboats and a nearby barge were a half-naked mob, with red bandanas tied on backward. Most of them were of mixed blood—Indians with a Spanish or Moorish cast of face, remnants of slave traders of Morgan's day. For Morgan and others had put in here, and there is still a song sung in Paraíso that tells of manacled oarsmen set free by the Chontales when they killed the Spanish and English pirates and burned their ships. The song still chills the blood, and its wild pride in the mixture of savage blood and the manacled galley slaves sets men to stamping in the cantinas and gives rhythm to the bodies of fishermen as they pull in their nets. Moorish eyes and hair; a Mayan nose; Mayan hands, quick and infinitely clever; a blue-black beard and grin from some Mediterranean ancestor of buccaneer days—these are the people of the Gulf coast from Campeche to Coatzacoalcos and Veracruz. They call themselves the Gallegos, insolently, full of themselves.

The *Deica* was listing slightly to one side, like a large hippopotamus eyeing the noisy newcomers with disfavor. The group of swarthy banditry grinned up at us, and a self-important port official in weatherbeaten cap and brass-buttoned coat shouted at our captain, demanding papers

125

and intentions. It was a little ridiculous to ask a boat stuck on a sand bar what its intentions were. Quite obviously it was not going anywhere very soon.

Our crew put a rope ladder over the side, and the little man climbed aboard, his mustaches bristling with importance. Almost at once he began berating everyone for everything.

Why did we do this? Didn't Captain Oleson know this was a dangerous channel? Who authorized him to come into Mexican waters? What business did he have here anyway? Didn't he know that it was necessary to notify authorities before he came into a Mexican port? His papers read Coatzacoalcos, not Frontera; why hadn't he gone there? Whose error? What banana company?

And quarantine. Everyone would have to be quarantined. And a woman and children on board! And if she wasn't Mrs. Oleson, who was she? Their papers had better be in order or Captain Oleson would be in trouble if they tried to land. In any case everyone would have to be quarantined.

Lucia and I, by this time seasoned travelers, stood behind Mother struggling with our snickers. We knew how these things went, and knew also that we would be on shore before the day was over. We had great faith in Mother's poise and her way of managing difficulties.

When the health officer lined us all up and began sticking a thermometer into each face without benefit of alcohol, the port master came to our rescue. He climbed on board just in time and stopped the quarantine and investigations officer. Face was lost and regained, feelings boiled and cooled several times in the twenty minutes of argument that followed, but at last the port master bowed us to the

126

ship's side. We were to be allowed to go ashore immediately, and he would send the tug with us.

When Mother asked if Papa was in Frontera, the port master looked serious. A man had come in, three days before, from Monte Cristo. He said that a man who had passed Don Ernesto Rateike's place said he had seen a man from Santa Ysabel who said that an Indian had gone through that way saying that the rivers were up and no one could cross the Michol. That meant, of course, that Papa could not get away from the plantation for another week at least. He had waited for our telegram from Galveston, and the rains had closed down.

Perhaps one who has not lived in tropical mountains will find it hard to understand just how there is no traveling once the rains start. A gray sheet of water and mist covers the hills, sealing them away as completely as if it were a solid barrier. Rivers rise and flood fifty-foot banks in a few hours' time. Streams become rushing rapids, carrying whole trees along, the river stones rolling and crashing together with a roar like a hundred gravel-crushers, and neither horse nor man can cross and live.

So news had traveled the three hundred miles by grapevine, and we knew that in our mountains the rivers were out of their banks and of course the telephone line was down.

Our port master hurried to reassure Mother. He would see to it that she had the best of care in Frontera, and if Don Guillermo did not come within the week, he would get her passage on the river boat to Monte Cristo, where Father could surely reach us. By this time Mother was resigned to such situations. She gave up to it, as she always did, smiling and thanking the port master. She managed to make him feel that it was of course unfortunate not to be met by one's husband, but that certainly the Señor would come when he could, and that with the help of good friends such as he, we would be all right.

We had to climb down the rope ladder, slippery with the slime of years and the sea. We hung out in space over undulating water, a rowboat uncertainly bobbing below. The green waves lifted it up one minute, and the next it was out of reach, away from the ship and far below. In that perilous moment when I hung from the slippery rungs, looking down at the dark water and the faces of the men who reached up laughing and shouting, I hardly knew which was the more dreadful, the full-bodied moving sea or the dark grinning faces with their broken teeth, the sweat and spray-soaked clothes, and the inevitable dirty red kerchiefs around their heads. I looked up to the row of faces leaning over the rail above me, felt my hands slipping, let go, and went downward into the waiting hands, the shouts, the strong smell of sweat, and the rough laughter, and was set down safely enough in the rocking dinghy.

Walking from the hot jetties up the sandy streets of the town to the only hotel, the Grand American, we saw everywhere evidence of the violence of revolution. The walls were pockmarked with bullet holes. Children ducked quickly behind doors or trees at the slightest sound of commotion. Although outwardly the revolution was over, it had been fomented in towns like these, and the ribald old Polo del Norte, a cantina next to the hotel, had to be patched together regularly, for its walls more than once staggered from constant riddling with bullets. All day and all night political arguments still raged up and down its

128

length, and if bodies didn't come flying out of its swinging doors, bullets did. The more decorous populace gave it a wide berth.

We hurried along in the blazing morning sun to the hotel. Even at this time of day there were shouts and songs in the Polo del Norte. Mother stepped off the sidewalk into the street to avoid its doorway. Behind us, grinning dock boys carried our trunks and suitcases. The Chinese proprietor of the Grand American Hotel thoughtfully gave us rooms on the opposite side of the building, where stray pistol shots would not penetrate, and brought us tall glasses of "icy tea" and lemonade.

Except for the British consul and his Costa Rican wife, there were no other English-speaking people at all in Frontera. It was a town of exiles and politicos biding their time in the provinces until some "unpleasantness" had blown over elsewhere, Chinese stranded in port and unable to leave, drifters who came from nowhere and had no place to go, promoters, gamblers.

The elite of the town were ranchers who came in every Sunday night to walk around the plaza and show off, to "present" themselves to the public, to do a bit of courting, drinking, and gossiping. The young blades drove their sweethearts around and around the sandy plaza streets in carriages pulled by matched horses, with another running alongside, strung with bells and jangling silver pieces. No one really could explain that extra horse, although some said it was to help train it to carriage use. It was a redundancy, an extra touch, a careless display of wealth, for only the handsomest and wildest horses were so used. They were usually unbroken two-year-olds, controlled by a leather leader-rein clanging with metal decorations.

"Controlled" is not exactly the proper word, for the animals were frightened by the noise their decorations made and by the orchestra music, and consequently pranced and dashed about to the peril of everyone.

Lucia and I were permitted to ride breathlessly around once or twice, wedged in between a handsome mustached youth in white and his embarrassed sweetheart. The side horse, a white one and quite beautiful, threatened at any moment to turn and rush back into the carriage, and the two other patient beasts kept stopping suddenly in mistrust and bewilderment, nearly tossing us out over their heads. It was a fine display of bravado on the part of horse and driver, but Lucia and I thanked him kindly and refused a second invitation.

In the center of the plaza on these nights, an orchestra with two marimbas and a great drum thumped and tootled and bleated Mexican Típica songs into the flower-scented and mosquito-laden air. Everything was calm and peaceful. Everyone looked delighted, languid, and slightly interested, in the accepted Latin fashion. But on our first evening in town, one pistol crack cleared the place. The orchestra disappeared as if swallowed by some mythical monster, instruments and all, down into the base of the turnip-topped pergola. We hurried for cover too, but nothing more happened, and in an hour everyone was back promenading, laughing, and talking. If there were any bodies they had been whisked out of sight. Most notable of all was the fact that no one mentioned the momentary "inconvience," just as in polite society one doesn't speak of a dish the cook just broke. It is swept up and tossed out, and that is that.

For four days we sat and waited in Frontera, and each

130

day was exactly like the other, slow, dreamy, and nothing to do but watch. In the afternoons I sat in the barred window of the hotel and watched people go by. At two and three o'clock, while the sun was still hot, only children selling sweets or fruit passed along. Their child-shrill voices echoed back from the walls: "Dulce, dulces. Frutas, frutas y dulces!" They stopped to smile shyly and offer a meringue through the bars for my ten-centavo piece. They stared at me and I at them, each envious of the other—they of my shiny black shoes and white dress, the envy of the free for the elegance they think means freedom; and I of the grace with which they moved, the liberty to walk barefooted and to carry sweets in a tray on one's head, the envy of the safe-pastured for the excitement of the hunt.

As the hot afternoons cooled into sundown, the movement about town increased. A small group of men passed the window, carrying a huge cayuco across town. It rested on their shoulders, their bronzed legs moving with bent knees in the swift dogtrot of the Chamula. With each step they kept up a rhythmic but soft "mmf, mmf, mmf." Up from the Gulf, they were carrying the cayuco to the Usumacinta. They would head on upstream to some unknown village in the interior. I watched them go, their loincloths white, their steps firm, their long black hair moving against their muscled shoulders, like characters out of a biblical pageant. They might not come to Frontera again for years, perhaps never. I knew the sort of places they were going, and once again I grew restless with the feeling that came at times like this—that other things waited while I stood thus in my childhood.

Some men and women from the southeast, wearing the

131

embroidered skirts and camisas of the Yucatan Mayas, walked slowly along, stopping every now and then to talk together. They stood across from the hotel and stared at me, not in astonishment, but rather in disbelief at what they saw. Their words, heavy with Mayan speech, exchanged ideas about me, but soon they lost interest and went away. I was a creature strange as something seen in a zoo, and they registered amusement and interest and went away with their easy walk and their straight backs and clean white huipiles, to see more of the town.

With the long shadows came the horsemen galloping or prancing by, spurs jangling, sombreros on the backs of their heads, sand flying out behind the horses' hoofs.

Two young men, walking their horses, stopped outside the window to light cigarettes and to "saludar" me, smiling and complimenting the "chiquita señorita." Their voices were deep and cultured, voices that had been to school in Mexico or Europe, speaking the tongue of the conqueror in this Indian land, with the mark of the provinces in their accents, swallowing the ends of their words like all Tabasqueños.

Then music, marimba and guitar, announced the beginning of the hour to promenade. The quick tropic dusk flushed a lavender-gray over the housetops, the far western sky deepened into dark magenta, and suddenly it was evening, with the Chinese in their black silk suits and their long queues standing out in the cool air by the lampposts. They stood silently, smoking their long-stemmed pipes, looking past the people who walked by, thinking their own thoughts of exile.

Children, clean and fresh even to the poorest, hair braided with bright ribbons even if they wore no shoes, began

132

running and playing in the park. Mother called, and we went to the plaza to watch the young men and their sweethearts, to smell the jasmine and gardenias, and to have a refresco of papaya at the little stand under the almond trees.

THE PEOPLE who live along the Usumacinta have silent faces. Their days are a ritual of the jungle and the river. They know some of the secrets it guards, for along its course lie the myriad remnants of a civilization long gone. Each day the waters wash more earth from its banks, and the sun rests on a bit of pottery or a carved household god that has been hidden for a thousand years. As the river gives up these secrets, the people look at them and hide them, thinking their own quiet thoughts. They say that some of these figures have a significance it is not good to look upon.

In the dark nights, inside the thatched huts with only the charcoal glow for light, the grandmothers tell of things that happened where the river now flows. They know that, where today they sleep in wattle huts with mud floors, there once were temples and palaces. They tell the children that the great plumed serpent of Ku Kul Kan became the river itself, wandering and twisting over the land. They remember that the river saw the bloody coming of the Nahua among the peaceful Maya, and the sacrifices they

134

brought. They know from history and legend of the Conquest, the buccaneers, and the black-robed friars. This river has heard the toll of golden-voiced bells, brought from Spain, calling the people from their ancient worship. It has seen the jungle, quiet, omnipotent, close over these things as surely as time itself absorbs that which is over and done. And now, at last, the river ironically tosses lost remnants of Mayan grandeur into the laps of the poor who live along its banks.

From Frontera we braved the river dreaming among its blossoms, profoundly deep at this turn, treacherously shallow at that. Up river we went, a two-day run to Monte Cristo. Our paddles churned the water behind us, spewing out foam and lily pads. Upstream, deeper into the wilderness, we wound through dense black stretches of forest where only wild parrots defied our passage.

The Usumacinta was more than a river to me, more than a way inland. Every turn was a familiar friend: the lush jungle, the creatures that slipped out of the forest to drink at its side, the shallows where reed and cattails grew and white herons, wings outspread, glided slowly over smooth backwaters, each shadow a cross upon the dark, still water. All these things and more: cornfields and banana groves, a cluster of palms hung with heavy fruit, and above, the fathomless blue sky piled billow upon billow with white gleaming clouds.

Can anyone who has not lived with the earth really know the meaning of going home?

There is a way of putting fetters on things, limiting their power by definition. Who, knowing the chemicals of the soil, can know the smell of it after rain? Querencia is called by many names—instinct, back-tracking, search for a return to pap-fed childhood. But home is not always a symbol of protection. Sometimes it is filled with danger, is uncertain, is full of things that would send others away. So the earth-querencia comes out of birth and death and ritual as old as man, and it pulls the blood of you to one special place and no other. It is there (wherever that there is) that you can hear something outside of yourself, and sometimes what sounds like destiny for man.

For the earth has a way of speaking aloud and holding all of you. Ever and always, home will be a feel to the sky, a look to the curve of a hill, a smell in the morning air. Those things will call you back, in search not of lost childhood but of something that went unanswered, that was left behind when you went away. Because you invariably leave something of yourself—in the house, in the earth, in the trees by the river. And these things will not leave you alone wherever you walk on earth.

Since she was part of this sort of thing, I must speak of Ragī. The Usumacinta that holds so many secrets, that has closed over many a Mayan wayfarer, priest, or burden-bearer, that has hidden many a gold headpiece, holds also my Ragī.

Ragī was a doll, a rag doll with very little face, no hair, and few clothes. She had never failed to comfort me in those lonely and terrible moments of doubt and dark that come to all children. She had traveled many times up and down the river with me. She had nodded from my saddle on long rides, and had lain soft and comforting in my arms when we slept in strange huts or under the canopy of the jungle.

Perhaps I was beginning to understand something of

136

the meaning that a limp symbol without form and face could have. Perhaps she was becoming something more than a creature of my invention wherein I could put my secret trust. The Karivís had shown me what a symbol meant. They had turned a leaf in my hand and shown me that things were important and had meaning only when clearly seen in full focus for what they were. They had shown me that reality was not the form or the fact, but the significance.

So it was that I began to look at Ragī with something more than casual acceptance. I sat and stared at her face, tracing in my mind where the eyes and nose and mouth were outlined. She was a little vague in her anthromorphic aspect. But her complete quiesence lying in my lap, her inability to sit up, her unresponsiveness, were all a sham. There was something terribly strong, something intense about her. She was an image, and I loved her and was angry with her all in the same moment. How could an image one loved be suddenly so inadequate? Why was I no longer content with the symbol, with the comfort of her limp rag arms? What did I need of her?

So, questioning, without thinking about it exactly, I tossed her at the cabin door, wanting to turn away from her but not really intending to separate us forever.

In that split second it happened. My aim was poor, and the swing of my arm carried her outward in the opposite direction. She went overboard, face up, down past a row of dark hands that reached out for her from the "steerage" as she fell into the river.

Knowing is something that comes slowly over a long period of time, and then suddenly one day it strikes the notes just right and a whole fanfare of violent understanding comes at once. That I had not meant to throw her overboard was beside the point. I had. That she was only a rag doll was unimportant also; the symbol remained.

For a horrible moment I thought she would be crushed in the whirling paddles behind the boat, but some trick of current carried her out, to drift all uncomplaining among the hyacinths and water tulips. I watched her until we turned a bend and she was lost to me.

There were three towns and perhaps twenty fincas in the entire distance to Monte Cristo, normally a two-day run. But our progress was slower, for at one of the riverside fincas the crew took French leave en masse to attend a fiesta. Passengers and officers were abandoned to the breathless heat, one night, two nights, while the deserters went two leagues away to wear themselves out with dancing and aguardiente.

During the time they were ashore the imprecations of everyone left behind produced some marvelously elaborate invectives, and as often as not included graphic descriptions of what was going to happen to them. But once all the impossible, hook-nosed, parrot-beaked, decrepit tapirs came on board, the captain did nothing—although of course his "You cat-tailed, two-toed, disemboweled anteaters" was said loud enough for all to hear.

Within an hour after their return we were under way, and Monte Cristo lay half a day ahead. We came upon the town quite suddenly around a bend and roused it from its afternoon torpor with a wild toot of our whistle. We saw a landing wharf, a big mercantile store, a plaza, a jail, and one grassy street lined with tile-roofed stucco buildings. Brilliant bougainvillaea, hibiscus, and flowering vines hung

138

over the blue and pink walls, and flamboyant trees grew along the riverbank. It was beautiful, but steamy hot and full of malaria. Like a gaudy, poisonous blossom it stood above us on a low bluff, suspended between green earth and blue sky.

In silence we hung along the rail to watch the boat slide into her mooring at steps cut in the red clay bank. Naked children ran down the grassy slope to stare, shy women stood back in the shade of the big open market by the mercantile store, their black rebozos drawn tightly over their sleek dark hair. Two men dressed in white got up from the coffee stand in the market, put on their peaked sombreros, and sauntered down to the landing. They stood there, feet apart, hands in pockets. No one spoke. Everyone watched and waited while the stilled paddles dripped and the water rippled between the boat and landing. A small group of men from the hills squatted on the bank, hair hanging long about their faces, elbows resting on knees, hands limp, mouths ajar with the intensity of their concentration on the strange contrivance that rode on the river. Everyone watched in silence, waiting in tableau for the thud of the boat against earth, the rush of bare feet, the slide of the plank, and the bustle of unloading to begin.

We stared at the people on the bank and they stared back. Our eyes searched the faces, hoping that Papa was there; but except for Don Pancho, a rancher from Tres Ceibos, we saw no one we knew. San Leandro suddenly seemed very far away, although now it was no more than eighty miles on horseback.

Before the ropes were made fast, at the exact moment the boat touched the shore, the owner of the mercantile rushed out as if he had been waiting for a signal. His black mustaches bristled, his revolver swung low from his hip, his voice echoed with imprecations against everything and everyone.

Who had done this! Why hadn't anyone done that! He was a mestizo, loud of voice and manner, and for that moment boss of the river. But no one resented him. The workmen simply exchanged glances, grinning a little wryly, and the villagers came closer to watch the show.

Two mahogany planks, set at steep angles from railing to shore, were the gangway. Hill Indians carried out the cargo, running bandy-kneed up and down. They staggered under enormous loads of flour and kerosene, cases of machinery and general store supplies. The planks vibrated with the thud of feet and the rock of the boat. We watched, fascinated, until finally a man under the fantastic load of a saddle, a sack of flour, and a can of oil lost his balance and teetered, swaying and gyrating. He thrust out his legs at odd angles, jouncing up and down, not daring to let go the load with either hand. Everyone on boat and shore began to shout encouragement and whoops of appreciation. They roared out advice and laughter in a dozen dialects until finally, grinning and floundering, the man and his load went into the river with a "Wahoo" and a splash.

"There goes your kerosene," one man called across to another. "No more sitting up to entertain yourself with your books and papers now, Don Miguel, you'll have to go back to love-making."

At that the whole bank roared with laughter, and in the shadows by the store the tittering women nudged each other and blushed.

The Indian fished himself out, rescued what he could of the lost load, and carried it, dripping and soggy, up to the

140

store. Mustaches was beside himself with fury, but the Indian only grinned, his head bowed under the weight on his back. He looked at his fellows from under his eyelids in a kind of secret pleasure. This time the joke was on the store-owner, for the load-carrier didn't take the loss.

We went ashore and sent the dock boys ahead with our suitcases. The trunks would have to come later. There was only one hotel in the town, and we went to it, walking through the plaza where the fruit and refresco vendors had opened their little shops and everyone was sipping and gossiping. Even the faces that peered from the barred jail windows were contented. They had ringside seats, and friends brought them fruit and stopped to chat, for it was a misfortune but never a disgrace to be in jail in these times when political affiliations were greater crimes than murder.

There was a big meeting of cattlemen in town, and dust swirled around the hoofs of horses galloping through the one main street. The men rode leaning half-out of their saddles to shout at friends, sombreros jingling with silver, spurs jangling, everyone showing off. It was not yet the hour when women were out on the street, and we hurried along, conscious of stares and of the rearing and plunging of horses suddenly turned in mid-gallop so that their riders could look at the gringas.

The hotel proprietor had a bland, fat visage that only became more bland and expressionless when Mother asked for rooms. He smoothed his mustache and shrugged.

"Of course I know a gentlewoman alone with two children has to sleep somewhere, but"—his hesitation hinted vaguely that we might have stayed home where we belonged—"my friends' wives stay on their plantations and are not permitted to go about the country."

Mother informed him coldly that it was none of his business why she traveled alone, but it was his business to provide accommodations to respectable people. If his hotel was filled with men, why didn't he double them up or send some of them elsewhere? Was Don Guillermo without friends here in Monte Cristo?

The manager shrugged. If the American señora was determined to have accommodations regardless, very well. He took up a large bunch of keys with a malevolent look at us and led the way. Mother followed with the little toss of her head we knew meant "situation in hand." My sister and I crowded close behind her, curious to see what was coming.

With a flourish the man opened a door and bowed us in. There were two empty beds, if the señora wished them!

The room was long and narrow and dark, lined with beds that were merely shelves against the wall with posts to support them. Seated on all but two of these were Mexicans in various stages of undress. A delighted ripple of comment and a few exclamations in Spanish welcomed us. The proprietor grinned toothily. He was sorry, but the señora had said she must have beds. He spread out his hands vaguely, his lower lip thrust out, his eyes more opaque than ever. One look was enough. We turned and fled down the narrow corridor to the hot sunlight outside.

There had been a quick squall and the street was still running water. We picked our way along toward the plaza, trying to avoid the deep muddy puddles. Mother held her heavy skirts up and admonished us to be careful of our shoes. Because of the sudden rain, the plaza was momentarily empty. We followed her to one of the concrete benches under the trees and sat down.

142

There were many times when living on a plantation in the jungle must have lost all glamour for Mother—times when her aloneness in this land must have been an affliction, when she remembered the concerts she loved, the opera, and the pleasure of sharing music that only fine musicians may have.

She sat wearily now, her hands idle in her lap. She looked past the tree-lined square with a wistfulness that sent me closer to her, to lean against her arm and stare into her face with a sorrow I did not understand. Sitting there on the bench, she became silent with such an intensity that we dared not break it. For perhaps an hour we sat there, an hour in which Mother did not move, and in patient lethargy we knew enough to keep her silence, although the bench grew hard and we were hungry and forlorn.

"Señora."

It was Bartolo, broadly smiling, standing erect and important, his hat twisting in his hands.

"Señora, Bartolo is here!"

What of Father? What of the storms and the trails?

The Michol bridge was out. He, Bartolo, was the only one to get across before it was swept away. He had promised Father he would find us, had ridden day and night, and here he was!

I suspect Mother listened to him with a grain of salt, but nevertheless the fact remained that Bartolo was there, however he had managed it. If he had said he crossed the river by swinging Tarzanlike on lianas, we would not have been surprised, knowing Bartolo's love of melodrama. As it turned out, he had already gone to Palenque ahead of the last storm and had reasoned that Father wouldn't get out, so had come on with a group of cattlemen hoping for a gay time in Monte Cristo and the good luck to find us, which happy event would save him from castigation. Technically, he was right. The bridge was out, he was the only one to get across, and he had promised Father (on an average of once a day for some years) that he would look out for us. Who were we to quibble over a discrepancy in the timing of events?

As soon as Mother explained the hotel situation he was off. He would arrange everything. And as a matter of fact he did, reappearing in half an hour quite triumphant. Like a magician taking a rabbit out of a hat, he had produced lodgings. We were to have a room, a very special room in a private home. It was large and had beds. We were to have privacy, and above all comfort. He, Bartolo, had done all this!

Mother's sense of humor had difficulty with Bartolo at times like this. In our dampened and weary condition his flourishes did not seem to offer very substantial hope. However, he had actually achieved the amazing luxury of a large room in a respectable house.

WE WENT into the
lamp-lighted house and met the owner, who bowed and all
but bumped his head on the floor in his eagerness to say his
home was ours. His wife, standing beside him, was a pale,
dark-eyed woman who smiled very little but brought Mother
coffee and cakes. We children ate the little cakes gratefully
and looked at a cabinetful of delicate china cups and little
brightly colored ceramic horses and bulls and gay toreadors.
The well-furnished living room was a strange mixture of
heavy provincial furniture and Louis Quinze chairs, relics of
the French influence in Mexico, brought from their home in
the capital city. A delicately carved marble-topped table
stood beside a ponderous mahogany settee and footstool. On
the walls were rococo gilt frames with startled, frigid-looking
people staring out of them, and on the tile floor were spread
jaguar skins. The most astonishing thing was a decrepit rose-
wood grand piano. When mother asked about it, the señora
sighed and said it was out of tune now, but her husband
had bought it for her when they were married.

"It's too damp for a piano here," she said. "We have to

keep a candle burning inside all the time against rust. But I like to remember when it was new and stood in our home in Mexico." And she looked paler than ever in her high-necked white tucked dress with the full sleeves.

Presently our host took us through a fern-hung patio to our lodging, a spacious, barren room with three beds. Two of them had high mahogany headboards, canopies, and mosquito netting. The other was a shelflike affair with bamboo for springs and a petate, a woven mat, for mattress. But it had clean sheets and white mosquito netting. I would sleep there.

The gentleman bowed. "At your orders," he repeated again and again. We were more than welcome. Anyone who came to him from Don Guillermo was always welcome, his own family most of all! We should never have gone to the hotel. Barbarians! All the people in this town were barbarians. Here we should have privacy. Indeed, he was indebted to us for permitting him to offer it to us.

Mother lasted long enough to be polite, and then when Bartolo had set our luggage inside the door and it was shut against the obsequious gentleman, she collapsed on the bed. Her last words to Bartolo had been a command.

"We are leaving here by six in the morning. You are to be here to help me. I shall not send anyone after you. If you are not here I shall get horses myself and go without you and you need never return to San Leandro."

Bartolo was hurt. Deeply hurt. How could the Señora doubt him so? He would be there. Indeed, he would even have the horses arranged for and have them at the house by six. He, Bartolo, would arrange everything. He left with an injured air that all too plainly spoke of Mother's ingratitude for his successful management of the lodging

146

problems. But at this point Mother was remembering Bartolo's love of conviviality, and she wanted no more problems about getting away. She laughed about it now as she opened our suitcases and hunted out our night things.

"He is really dependable, you know," she said to us, taking down the long chestnut-dark coil of hair and holding the tortoise-shell pins in her mouth, "but it doesn't do to speak softly to him. He thinks I don't mean it. Well, we'll see. But someway, girls, we will be on our way in the morning."

It did not take us long to undress, but before we were done there came a loud knock at the door. With many and profound apologies the owner of the house entered, carrying a long pole on the end of which hung a large hunk of raw meat. Huddling behind our mosquito netting, we watched him proceed through the room to a door that we had not previously noticed behind a large chest of drawers. He pushed the highboy to one side and, gingerly opening the door a crack, thrust in the pole with its burden of meat. When he withdrew it the meat was gone, and he quickly pulled the door closed and returned the chest to its position.

He turned to us with an embarrassed look. "A little animal," he said apologetically, "a poor little beast. A man has bought him for the zoo." He overflowed with excuses. We would not be disturbed again. It was really much better to feed the poor little thing, lest it cry in the night and annoy us. He bowed himself out, and we heard his feet scuffing down the corridor like the white rabbit hurrying to the Duchess.

Mother looked at the chest of drawers for some time without saying anything. We were all thinking the same thought. Any animal that could devour that enormous

147

chunk of meat could not be such a poor little thing. My sister and I got up to investigate and found that there was no latch or lock on the door, but we reported that the high-boy was secure. Since the door opened into the other room, we could swing it inward with a little push, but with the highboy there we decided that nothing could get at us, even if it could pry the door open. There were no sounds coming from the room, so we went back to bed and to sleep.

I think we all must have awakened at about the same time. Some sound made me sit up and listen.

Moonlight coming through the barred window back of my bed spread out over the floor. I could see through the mosquito netting into the dark room and the square of light with its stripes of shadow. There, within a few feet of me, stood a large jaguar, sleek and mottled and terrible. It was not at me that he was looking. His eyes were focused beyond me, up toward the window and freedom. The light gleamed into his wide eyes and made satin the flat top of his dark head. I must have moved, for in that second he crouched and looked at me, holding himself poised, waiting. A jungle-trained child knows what to do. I sat still, melting myself into the shadows of my bed, becoming nothing, giving out neither fear nor presence. For that much I had learned from the Indians—how to become nothing, to negate myself, so to speak, so that no presence could reach out to the delicate radar of wild creatures. Only human odor could give me away.

But the jaguar was not hunting. He was not concerned with humans, for he was trapped. No food, no enemy was so important as the bars that stood between him and the moonlight outside. Sitting there, huddled a little, I began to feel sympathy for that great creature; I began to under-

148

stand the terrible desperation, the call from outside the window that was greater than fear or hunger. Perhaps it was because his eyes looked directly at me and mine back at him that the awareness began to grow.

There are few times when a jaguar full grown looks directly and fully at a man. A child has not the hundred barriers built up in him to repel animal eyes. So we stared at each other, and I felt something of what had surrounded me the night I ran down alone to the Karivís across the river. I knew what purity and terrifying innocence lay in wild creatures. I knew the tremendous call that came to them. I knew, because in me existed the same thing, the unthinking purity and flight of spirit when enwrapped in "the law of the heart," which exists in all creatures. And now, in these brilliant eyes that looked at me full of misery, I knew the panic of being lost from all the comforting freedom of that law. I knew the creature's aching sorrow, separated from his place.

I remembered what the Karivís had told me of how love is: as real as the moonlight, as sure as the space above our heads, but as fragile as the colors a prism makes. You cannot hold it, but all of you rushes to meet it when it calls, and there is no loss more great than when it goes from you. I would always remember these things, and the jaguar's eyes.

All this was only a moment, an oblivion to everything else, for Mother's shout must have come almost immediately, and the instinctive reaction of a trapped animal flexed the jaguar's muscles. He crouched lower, breathing heavily with a throaty sound, a low gurgle deep down. His eyes shifted to the window, and I could feel the fright in him spread out like a dye of hatred and fear. In times like this,

149

when a child sits so close to those things he cannot dim with adult rationalization, he becomes aware beyond his understanding. So it was that I shared the jaguar's violence, and I shrank back.

"Throw your shoes at the door, pound on the walls!" Mother commanded us. "Shout for help!"

The door opened. Our host put his head in, took one look, and slammed it shut again. The jaguar backed away, then turned and retreated into the dark room beyond the highboy. We all jumped at once to push it close against the door and scrambled back to bed. In a few minutes the man opened the door again and stuck his head inside. Mother asked him to please secure the door in better fashion, and he came in, mopping his brow, covering himself with abuse for his carelessness. Why, we might all have been eaten!

"Yes," Mother answered dryly, "we might have."

WHEN WE AWOKE to morning, the first thing we heard was Bartolo outside our window bargaining for some pan dulces. Bartolo was there! And it was only seven o'clock. True, he was a little drunk, but he had achieved the impossible: horses, good-looking beasts too, and the baggage already loaded on mules. The reason for this miracle was simple. Bartolo had placed himself in jail. He had used the practical ruse of saying the Don Guillermo requested it, and his good friend the jailer, who had locked him up often enough on less pleasant occasions, was delighted to comply. Of course all his friends had joined Bartolo, and they had a gay time through the night, their only concern to keep the jailer sober enough to get Bartolo out by six in the morning.

The sun was always brutal on the open campos after seven. Usually no one started out after three in the morning, so he could cross to the hills and forests before ten. But Mother wanted to go only a few hours from town, as far as the Aguacate, a ranch halfway to Palenque.

From the Aguacate there was hope of an easier journey.

Father had written to us in the States that Don Ernesto had a new wagon and he would send it through to the halfway ranch to pick us up. There was a new bridge over the Chevi Chivol and Santo Domingo arroyos, and the cart could go across the grasslands without a road. Mother joked about it and promised us a chariot. But she eagerly looked forward to release from the long, jogging horseback ride, hours upon hours of it, that lay ahead. From the Aguacate it was still five hours' hard riding to Palenque town, and starting as late as we were from Monte Cristo, we would do well to get to the halfway point by late afternoon.

There were two dangerous spots on the trail—the dye woods and the jaguar campos. In mating season it was foolhardy to cross those open fields at night. During the brama the animals became ferocious, fighting and choosing mates up and down the broad grasslands, hiding only when morning brought day and heat. The dye woods was a dangerous crossing of a river that frequently went completely out of its banks with the first rains.

There was another place too, beyond the Aguacate and the jaguar campos, that no one liked to pass after dark. It was the bell woods. These woods were an arm of jungle that jutted into the campos, swallowed the trail for a mile or two, and was difficult, day or night. Mudholes in rainy weather were a problem, and superstition hung heavy about this stretch and made men erratic and things go wrong. When you are sitting safely in your chair at home, it is hard to understand just what superstition can do. Fireside travelers may curl their lips all they please, but sometimes the bell woods took courage, even though there was nothing anyone could see. The trail that cut through them was the old route used during the Conquest. Before that

152

it had been an Indian trail, the route of travelers since early peoples went from the Usumacinta to the mountains beyond Palenque.

In the days of the Spaniards, when the trappings of the Church were carried in, a tremendous bronze bell on an oxcart sank into the mud in these woods. The men, working furiously to move the cart out of bottomless mire, fell to quarreling, so the story goes, and were an easy prey to a band of robbers, who killed them all, including an innocent priest. They stole all the goods but the bell, which they could not carry away, and left the men lying in their own blood in the woods. Those who pass there now leave lighted candles in the trail for the souls of the departed, so that living men may go in peace. But even the most daring will not go through there near midnight, for they say the bell tolls most dolefully, and if a man hears it and forgets his Aves, he is doomed.

We would ride horseback through the first of the campos and cross the dye woods before we came to the Aguacate. The river at the dye woods was out of its banks, as we knew it would be, the bridge under water, and there was an hour's delay in the heat while Bartolo went upstream to look for an Indian family that might have a cayuco.

When the dye woods river went out it was no small affair. It flooded the grasslands on either side for a mile or more. The woods, with water up along the trunks almost into the branches, were sullen and sinister, for these trees that colored the water were also poisonous to most birds, and were dark and uninhabited.

We punted into the shadows of the trees, and I sat very still in the dugout. The cayuco was loaded until water slipped over the edges in little trickles. We sat on our saddles and leaned back where the tree branches were low. The mottled world of the woods around us was silent. The boatmen bent their lithe bodies this way and that to counterbalance the thrust of their poles, crouching low under the limbs, pushing us along, their eyes watchful. Once a streak of bright coral red moved beside the cayuco. Bands of black and yellow decorated the long, thin body of a snake. The flat venomous head moved within a foot of my hand on the cayuco edge. The boatmen crossed themselves and exchanged glances, for it was an omen they did not like, but the snake stayed with us, gliding easily along until we were almost out of the woods. Then it slipped away through moss and liana, a fantastic thin line of color on the opaque dark water.

We could hear Bartolo up ahead shouting at the horses. "Whup, whup, whup," his voice came back to us through the trees. It was a difficult, long, and dangerous swim for the horses. Floating logs and trailing vines were everywhere, the most open passages full of debris. When we got out into the sunlight on the other side of the woods, we found that two of the horses had run away and one of the mules was rolling on his pack of luggage trying to get it off. Because of the snake, the boatmen said.

By the time the horses were caught and saddled, a storm came blowing up out of the Gulf behind us. One moment the sunlight was hot and bright; the next, a cloud passed overhead and the sudden wind ripped at our hair and clothes and pressed down the tall campo grass. The sullen woods lay behind us. Before us the yellow-green campo spread lurid in the half-light of the racing storm.

Bartolo pulled at the leather thongs that held our rubber ponchos to our saddles. His head was bent into the wind,

154

his peaked sombrero tipped to protect his face from its fury. Then we were in the saddles, our capes, smelling of rubber, hot and sticky about us.

As on the sea in a hurricane, the air became still, sucked dry of motion, of density. It was hard to breathe; we were flattened and empty as though the campo lay cupped in a vacuum. In the thick, silent heat we felt the blood pounding in our ears, while the storm gathered to rush at the earth, sealing sky and ground together in gray sheets of rain.

The first great clap of ear-splitting, racking thunder was a relief. The rain came from behind us, engulfing us in torrents of water. We could see only jagged lightning running into the ground beside us, in front of us. All about was the strange hissing sound of rushing, wind-driven rain. The horses moved forward slowly, heads down between their front legs, stepping unevenly in water that was already ankle deep on the trail. I could scarcely see the form of the horse in front of me, with the cape and peaked sombrero of Bartolo looming over it in the pounding rain. We knew enough to keep our heads down, for the whipping wind drove rain under our hats, soaking our faces and hair, and if we lifted our heads even a little, we were instantly blinded by the rushing water.

Only two courses are open to the wayfarer caught in such a storm: to revel in it, to go with it, driven before the wind willingly, sharing the wild uproar; or to cringe close to the ground somewhere, shuddering before every thunderclap, trembling with each new streak of lightning, wrenched by sound and wind, beaten upon by stinging rain. But there is no safety. Not anywhere. The open campo is terrifying and dangerous, and the jungle offers little protection, for although the wind is lessened, trees fall with their burden of rain-soaked termite nests and sodden branches. The trail becomes a bog, sucking at the feet of horses, dragging them in to flounder to their saddle girths in a quagmire of slippery black clay.

For five hours we rode through the afternoon, while the storm wore itself out against the mountains ahead and darkness began to move its mauve shadows across the grass. At the Aguacate ranch we dragged ourselves off, exhausted, to stumble into the thatched house, grateful for the quiet and the welcome smell of corn coffee, the charcoal fire, and a great pot of steaming tepesquintla stew. There had been some hope that Father would at least meet us here, but Don Alberto shrugged at our dismay. He had heard nothing except that a man who passed the day before said that he heard from an Indian from the hills that Don Guillermo had already left San Leandro. But where he might be now was a question. "The Michol is out, you know," Don Alberto said, as if that explained everything.

The wagon was there, however. It had been waiting a week for us, so at least that plan had gone through.

It was wonderful to sit out under the ramada in the back court with plates of hot tepesquintla, sliced avacados, and papaya before us, while the smiling folk shook their heads and clacked their tongues at our getting through the storm at all. The parrots sitting on the roof beams muttered their own opinions. They kept their bills snug behind their red and green wings, only their bright, interested eyes, yellow and red and yellow again, showed that their guttural mutters were waking comments on the intruders.

Kerosene lamps swung from the ramada and shed a mellow light into the rain-filled darkness outside. Scrawny dogs stretched asleep after the first investigations, and a

156

small pig, tied to the table leg at our feet, grunted his disapproval of the storm, the dogs, and the guests.

There was considerable talk about whether we should go on or stay. The woods were bad and the carreta road might be dangerous, but there was no place for us to sleep at the Aguacate. The ranch house was a large thatched dwelling with earth floor and two rooms. There were no beds, and the only hammocks were those that belonged to Don Alberto and his family. So when at eight o'clock Don Alberto reported that it was clearing and some stars were out, Mother said "Good, let's go on." There would be a moon to light us across the jaguar campos, and Don Alberto agreed to go with us for added protection.

I watched the lantern swing through the dark corral to the shed where the horses and mules were huddled, and excitement at the nearness of San Leandro woke me up. Out there in the darkness was our wonderful buckboard "chariot," and now we were only two days from home.

It was full night when we left the Aguacate. The moon was not due for an hour, but the campos were visible in a dim way, for the storm had passed and the sky was filled with stars. We were all terribly tired, but the novelty of going in a wagon keyed us up for a while. It was strange enough to go bouncing along over the campos with the team of mules trotting along efficiently, but it was a disappointment. Mother sat rigid. Her back was raw from hours of rubbing against the high, narrow saddle back all the way from Monte Cristo. And our chariot turned out to have no springs at all. The few oxcarts that used this "road" moved in a snail-like fashion over hummock and ditch alike, but this modern creation was never intended for passage over grasslands. It was made for hay loads, not campos in the dark. It was bad enough for Lucia and me, bobbing and bouncing along, but every jolt—and there was no cessation of jolts—must have wracked Mother's body and spirit.

In its right place a buckboard can be a much respected vehicle. And in its right place a mule is a much valued creature. But mules hate mud, and in tribulation are wont to moan and puff and blow in horrible fright and self-pity. Besides, we had made an error that many people made. Just back from the physical comforts of the States, we thought wagons and such better than riding horseback. The jolt of realization was as severe as the jolt of each wheel turn, and we soon subsided into a disconsolate silence and saw and thought of nothing but the black encircling forests and the miles and hours ahead. I am sure that at this point Mother felt she could bear nothing more, but the bell woods proved our complete undoing.

The dark, water-soaked jungle was still dripping from above and soggy below. It was impossible to guide the mule team around the worst mudholes, for there was no opening through the mat of forest on each side. Twice a mule floundered belly deep in the black clay before we finally came to a complete stop. With a lurch, one wheel sogged down until it was below the hub, and we were stuck at a forty-five-degree angle. The frightened mules pulled and plunged, wild-eyed in the lantern light, and one of them finally broke loose and went racing down the trail, its flying hoofs throwing a splatter of mud over us as it ran. The lantern was knocked out of Bartolo's hand and went out, he fell in the mud, and the remaining beast lay down in the traces. We could hear the mule wheezing heavily in the peculiar despair of mules in trouble, and

Bartolo's solid curses as he tried to pull the animal up. Lucia leaned over and whispered to me, "If we stay here long enough, we'll hear the bell toll." It was too dark for me to see her knowing wink.

Don Alberto climbed off the wagon and went to help. The matches he struck were tiny, ineffectual flickers in the blackout. While he hunted for the lantern, everything came to a stop and we sat still in the jungle darkness. Into the silence there crept also an awareness of the nameless listening creatures, real and imagined, that peopled the dark forest about us. We could feel their curiosity as their sensitive nostrils asked questions of our presence. We heard their amusement when a stir in the branches overhead broke the stillness and an unmistakable guffaw startled us. We could see nothing, of course, but once again from somewhere above we heard the amused "Ha hok! Ha hok!"

At such times as this all the rationalization one can muster does not obliterate the feeling that some half-human is watching and laughing. The jungle has its own ways of tormenting the intruder, and this is one of them. No use to tell ourselves that the voice was that of a sleepy toucan, the big-billed comedian of the forest; no use to remind each other that the stories of fearsome things that happened in the woods when the gogols laughed were only superstitions. We listened uneasily while the derisive "Ha hok, ha hok" grew fainter and at last ceased altogether.

Up ahead Don Alberto got the lantern going again, and a small yellow flame glowed. The mule lurched to his feet whistling and Bartolo shouted, "Tigre!"

Don Alberto held the lantern up, still, not moving, and we all stared into the black that surrounded us, not knowing where the jaguar might be. It moved slowly, and we saw

159

it about ten feet away, its eyes two gleaming evil lights with no expression in them, oblongs of yellow-green painted against the black forest.

This was very different from the creature we had seen shut in the room at Monte Cristo. This thing was predatory, hating us, watchful. My sister's frightened crying as she clung to Mother, Mother's tightening hands upon me, and the fear in Bartolo's voice acted upon me as violently as though I were actually being eaten alive, and I began to scream. Once I had begun, nothing could stop the fear that came to me from my mother and sister, built in me, and propelled shriek after shriek from my throat. The jaguar's gleaming eyes winked out and it vanished into the darkness, leaving only the acrid, nauseating odor that one never forgets.

My howls increased my sister's crying, the mule began a frenzy of kicking, and to add to everything it began to rain again. However Mother felt about it, she didn't say anything, but tucked the rubber poncho around my shoulders and put my waterproof hat on firmly, a good bit more firmly than was needed to make it stay.

I was still screaming some minutes later when a halloo up ahead shut off my yells as quickly as they had started. Another halloo came again to reassure us, and our fears and apprehensions were gone. Into the uncertain circle of lantern light rode my father, with Don Ernesto peering out of the dark behind him. Anxiety was in Father's face, but in his arms a few minutes later there was laughter for me.

"At least," he said, pulling my pigtails, "at least there was no doubt about where you were!"

Once we got to Don Ernesto's the world seemed good

again. We sat around his big dining table, laughing now that the trip was done, telling and retelling the things that had happened. Doña Petrona, the cook, brought steaming cups of coffee and hot chocolate and a platter of scrambled eggs and sausages with hot toasted tortillas and jam. We feasted at one in the morning, then took stock of our luggage and fell into dreamless sleep in the big comfortable beds.

Two days later we were in our saddles again, gratefully on our own sure-footed and well-turned-out horses, riding the long hours to San Leandro. This time I rode slowly, behind everyone, looking at and loving every great leaf, every secret shadow, and singing softly, "How many miles to Babylon? . . . Will we be there by candlelight? Aye, and home again."

THE STORMS that came down from Don Juan Mountain were violent, rending the trees with sudden, twisting gusts of wind, slashing at the leaves, beating everything to the earth. They were different from the plains storms. The canyons split and crackled with lightning, and the Duum rocked and rolled and echoed its thunder in the ravines.

Feliciana said the storms from Don Juan were the angry gods wreaking vengeance on the world, and that one must stay inside and cower under things lest the breath of their fury reach into the soul. She went around the house covering all the mirrors with cloths or pillow slips.

"Mirrors draw lightning," she whispered with a knowing look. "The angry gods hate to see themselves, they are so ugly, and they always send shafts to break mirrors. If a mirror reflected the face of the storm even once, we would all die."

But Charlie blew at his rice tray and squeezed his eyes up small and said nonsense, the winds and sudden storms were only the results of laughter. A little terrible, of course, but

162

none the less the laughter of the fate gods, who sometimes laughed so hard the earth shook, because man was such an incredible fool.

When he said that, I went and played the wind-up phonograph turned to loud, and listened to the storm music from *Wilhelm Tell,* and swung in the string hammock on the porch. Then I could see the length of the village, with its wet houses and grass and bandstand, as through a gauze curtain. The rain cut across it in wind-driven slanting sheets, bending the palm trees, bowing the heads of those who ran for shelter.

I had seen people worship in so many ways that it was hard to know where anyone found God. But worship was worship, and it had to have a feeling of wonder and revelation or it wasn't anything. I had been taught a reverence for a personal God by my father, Calvinistic severity by my aunts and uncles—"One doesn't run on Sundays." I had sensed something sacred in the candlelit quiet of cathedrals and convent chapels, had been aware of a kind of reverence in the pillared, marble-floored banks where everyone spoke in low tones, and had seen Charlie's teakwood prayer altars and smelled the sanctity of heavy incense before them. But most real to me was the Karivís' intense awareness of something omnipresent and divine, for this I myself could feel. About all the others there was something that repelled me, that I didn't understand, as if people and their minds got in the way too much.

Legends and superstitions fell into their own patterns of whimsey and fear. And witchcraft as such had never seemed very real. Lucia and I knew some of the local beliefs—that when someone was sick an ill wind had passed over his house, and that if a woman had a pain or went blind it was

163

due to the patatus, the leaping of a snake spirit into her. And we knew there were dark, occult thinkings about a woman when the moon was full, and that her husband would never take her to wife again if she stayed at the river after dusk, for in that case a duende would bewitch her and all her children would be born with pointed ears and teeth. We knew about making images and sticking pins in them too. But it was hard to believe anyone really meant any of those things. They were a way of speaking, that was all.

And now, after two years in places unknown, Don Lencho was suddenly back in our village, as though the storms had brought him. Father promptly made a rule against any more "soul-purging" and insisted on examining all his ollas of herbs, but it was difficult to keep him entirely away from the people. We never talked of these things, but we all knew that he was practicing his dark prognostications and séances and that most of the village believed in him. With his coming the whole place was changed somehow, there were unrest and uneasiness everywhere. I longed for the rains to be done and the Karivís to come again.

Don Lencho chose a new site for his incantations. It was a narrow, steep canyon across from the ceiba tree where the Karivís had stayed. There in a small clearing in the heavy forest he had a thatched hut, with a few dried peppers and an animal skull or two hung on the walls. But all houses had their trophies of javalí skulls or jaguar remains and teeth hanging about, so his place didn't look unusual to the passer-by. Nonetheless, we children were forbidden to go near it.

One afternoon while everyone still slept during the siesta hour—it was a dark day with only intermittent sun after a

164

rain—I went out back to see what Charlie was doing. There was no movement in the kitchen, and a wisp of blue smoke was coming from behind the partition. I knew Charlie was inside smoking his long pipe and would not hear me even if I called, so I turned away.

Then I heard a rolling sound welling up in the distance —whether the last of the thunder in the mountains or the throb of drums I did not know, but I decided to go and see. I walked across the yard, around the bathhouse, behind the chicken-yard fence, and slowly across fallen leaves through a small patch of woods to the undergrowth near the canyon. A great shadowy space lay behind me, between me and the safety of the chicken-yard fence. The rolling sounds were more plain now, and I knew they were made by drums.

I went the way the Karivís had taught me, slipping easily through the bushes. But this time a kind of hypnotized curiosity was leading me where I knew better than to go. This was forbidden ground, and every step took me deeper into a sense of guilt. A streak of sunlight lay far up on the tops of the trees. Mote-filled beams sifted down on the leaves in front of me. But when I reached the spot the sunlight touched, it had already shifted and was somewhere else. Like a tiny flashlight beam moved by an invisible hand, it searched through the thick foliage in the dusk where I walked, as if looking for some tiny thing in the overwhelming green.

Now there was a new sound mingled with the soft, swift rolling of hands on drums. It was a low "Hu eeya, hu eeya," and sometimes a moan broke into the rhythm and drifted off on the drumbeats.

I could see the hut, but nothing that was happening. Slowly I went down the slope, digging my heels into the

165

soft earth. Can anyone who has not heard it know the urgency in the quick smother of hands on drums? Like racing heartbeats; a forward pressure, fast, endless, beating out a life or a death. I lost my footing and slid, bumping into the back of the hut with a thud.

There was a cry, and the drums stopped. Instantly I was confronted by a woman and a man, angry, glaring at me. The man's face was painted—purple lips, red eyelids, and streaks of ocher on his temples. The woman was Marcelina's mother, her face screwed up in a terrible toothless rage. She shook her fist and screamed at me, and suddenly I wasn't afraid any more. Here was Don Lencho looking like the painted Judas the people chased out of town every year before Easter. It was only the drums that had made me afraid, some quality in their sound; but they had stopped. Besides, I knew enough not to show fear in front of these people. They knew who I was. So I glared back at them and demanded, "What are you doing?"

A moan inside the hut sent Don Lencho and the old woman back into its shadows, and suddenly the drumbeats began again. In front of the door hung long strings of corn and beetles, large ones with iridescent wings. Inside I could dimly see a woman standing, her arms upraised. She was holding onto ropes suspended from the ceiling, her head thrown back, naked except for a dark blue skirt that hung to her ankles. Two women held the ends of a rebozo wrapped tightly around her swollen belly. They pulled downward, and each time they did so the woman bent her knees and moaned. The drums hurried faster and faster under the hands of a half-grown boy, and the old woman and Don Lencho chanted and crouched, moving colored stones about in front of a small fire. It was unbelievable,

166

and yet something was happening that I did not understand—something that was powerful and solemn, bigger than Don Lencho and his chants.

In a sudden panic, I began to stamp my feet, hardly knowing what I was doing. "I'll stop it, I'll stop it," I thought. "I'll make my own magic."

I pulled some small cedar splinters from a niche in the wall and put them together in a T cross with some bits of liana, as the Karivís had taught me. In a moment more I pushed earth in the doorway into a small pyramid and put my cross on it. Then, knowing it would startle and infuriate the old man in the hut, I drew another T with a curved sky over it—Itzamná's own sign—in the ground just outside the door, screamed out "Don Lencho!" and ran.

Back in our garden I sat and stared at the flowers, the good clean earth and sky. A lizard was sunning himself on a white stone. Charlie had come to the doorway of the kitchen, sorting onions. Wild parrots flew over, jeering and laughing defiance at all but themselves, and the afternoon sun splashed bright on the breadfruit tree. But I knew what I knew and had seen what I had seen, and I put my head into my arms and was afraid. There was something in Don Lencho's presence at the finca that was like a dark cellar full of horrible things, and I was overcome with a knowledge I did not want to have.

At supper Sabatán the houseboy whispered, "I saw you." He grinned and looked slantwise out of his Bachajón eyes, and I was frightened all over again. "You'll see," he whispered again, clearing the table. "Marcelina is having a baby and it will be a brujo, a witch. You be careful or you'll have one too!" And he wagged his head with awful emphasis. "They'll stand all their saints on their heads after what you did today." He left me sitting with my mouth dry and the rice pudding untouched. I stole a look at Mother and Father, but we had company that night and they didn't seem to notice.

I did not blow out the candle at bedtime until Lucia made me, saying she would tell me ghost stories and scare the liver 'n' lights out of me if I left it burning. So I lay in the dark thinking about what I had seen. I did not know that Indian women always stood so to have their babies, but it wasn't Marcelina that had frightened me. It was the drums and the feeling of something wrong where there should have been something right.

Two days later Mother insisted on taking a new dress to Marcelina's baby. She said we should all go down to the village together to welcome the new inhabitant. From house to house we went, Mother in her soft white dress with the high lace collar. She carried a hat and a parasol, and we followed sedately behind, dressed in our best afternoon frocks. Smiling and nodding, Mother looked in at this house, paused to talk to the women at that one. From each doorway came the warm rich odor of roasting corn and fresh smoke. The small boys looked stiffly uncomfortable in their clean, unused pants and shirts; the women stood respectfully, their dark blue skirts pulled tightly around their waists, their spotless white blouses embroidered in bright colors neatly tucked in. Their hair was smooth and black, parted in the center and hanging in long braids or looped up in a beautiful kind of knot and held with one bright comb.

Marcelina lived at the far end of the village, near the store. As we went into her house I saw a candle burning secretly behind the door, and over the lintel hung a wreath of seed pods, rattling in the small breeze. I looked back longingly to the hot sunlight outside, to the shimmers of heat that rose from the wide avenue of green and the houses and coconut trees that quivered in the heat. I was afraid to look at the new baby, but Mother held it up for us to see. It had on a bright blue silk cap, to keep off the evil eye. Its little closed-up eyes made a secret of its face, and its tiny hands clasped nothing. But on its wrist was a band of colored threads, and from them hung a drop of pure amber shaped into a small figure. Two candles burned before an altar in one corner of the room, and there enshrined was the Virgen del Carmen, smiling at us. There was no sign of Don Lencho's machinations, for this was Domotilo's house, and in spite of Marcelina's beliefs Lencho did not dare set foot in it.

I suppose I was surprised that the baby looked like a baby and not a monster of some sort. But it was another thing to look at Marcelina. She lay inside a bed hung with mosquito netting, a bed made of bark with a woven mat on it. She was smiling in a pleased sort of way, but I had trouble looking at her. I hung back, guilty with my knowledge, afraid to look at the ribbons and signs festooned on the netting.

Mother praised the baby and left a little dress and a piece of goods as a present. She was careful not to praise it too highly, because these people believed you could bring them evil with flattery. But the present was received happily, to be made into a wrap. Then Mother asked what the child would be named.

"It has no name," said Marcelina in her soft, sly voice. "It cannot be named until the eighth day."

"The priest will be here soon now. This is his month for

169

coming," Mother answered. "You must have a name by then."

"We will call it Narcín when the time comes, and if it lives." Marcelina answered defiantly, afraid that anticipation, like flattery, would put a hex on the child. "We do not need the priest; this one was born with a special sign."

Everyone knew that the priest came to San Leandro once a year, and sometimes when things were bad once every two years, to marry the people who had been living together and to baptize the babies. It would soon be Christmas, and a padre would come. I wondered if Don Lencho would really dare say anything against the baptism. I knew the priest would send him away from the finca and excoriate the people if he knew the things that had happened.

When Marcelina brought the baby to the house for its presentation to the casa grande, it was a week old. I burned two candles for safety behind the front screen door, so nothing evil could come in with her.

After they had put out the fire, I looked ruefully at the black scar of charred wood by the door, listening to my father's words.

"You do not have to be afraid like this of anything, Catarina. Burn your candles on altars, if you wish, but not behind doors."

But I think he understood that I had been a witness to the ill wind that had already begun to blow dangers into this place.

OUR FIRST ALARM rode in during the siesta hour, when the finca common was empty, asleep in the pall of stagnant warmth that lay over it. Shimmers of heat made a blur of the houses, and nothing moved.

In the midst of our drowsiness, a drumming of hoofbeats pulled us upright, listening. Only danger or tragedy ever rode like that in the heat of the day. By the time the rider came racing through the finca gate, Father was already at the door. The horse, roweled and bleeding, foaming and dripping sweat, staggered to a stop in front of the casa and stumbled to its knees. The rider, with a rasping shout, slid to the ground and fell prone upon the grass.

The whole village came pouring out of dark doorways, hurrying to see what had come like this to San Leandro. Mariano ran to lead the horse away, to walk it up and down and save it if he could. My sister and I hung onto the garden gate to watch.

Father shook the man and rolled him over, but all any of us could understand was a hoarse call for aguardiente.

When a good swig had been poured down his throat, he managed to shout "Revolucionistas" in a revived voice, then immediately collapsed. More brandy.

"Viva la revolución! Two hundred men!" They were already at Lumija, burning and pillaging. He waved his arms, ready to get up and ride on, but gave up suddenly and fell back on the grass in a heavy sleep, quite sodden with brandy and exhaustion.

"Revolucionistas" might mean anything. The revolution was over; Díaz had fled and Francisco Madero governed as president in the capital; but the country still swarmed with armed and rootless men. Having discovered, as most revolutionists do, that the big promises of equality and fraternity were going to materialize only slowly, if ever, they turned their fighting experience into a means of livelihood. Bands of them went through the provinces looting and burning in a sweep of terror, and we heard increasing rumors of a new "capitán" with some two hundred followers who was cutting a swath of destruction through Tabasco and Chiapas. They were ripe for the bribery of guns and liquor offered by people like Henich, who used them to get rid of personal enemies.

Terrifying stories were told of these marauders. We heard of men dragged from their beds and thrust head-first into the five-foot hills of fire ants. There were drunken brawls in the villages, in which men and women were marched before the raiders, to be killed or spared as the whim struck. But we were so far from main-traveled roads that it still did not seem such a thing could come to us. San Leandro had the reputation in all Chiapas of being a rich and well-provisioned plantation, but Papa depended on two things for our safety. First, it was well known that we had given asylum to the families of many of these same men who were now going berserk in the land they had set out to free. Second, the long ride from Palenque or Salto probably would cool off any bandits before they reached us.

And, of course, as he pointed out, this alarm could be just another of Henich's tricks. When he went to try the telephone and found it dead, we were all sure Henich was at the bottom of the scare. This conviction grew stronger as several weeks passed without incident. But there was always the uneasy possibility that it wasn't Henich at all.

Then one evening came an urgent telephone call from Don Ernesto. The capitán was on the loose and heading our way. We could do nothing but run for it.

"Get everything ready tonight," Papa said, turning from the phone. "We'll leave at three in the morning." So there was bustling about, Mother packing the silver by candlelight, with the curtains drawn so our activity could not be seen from the village. The pieces gleamed in the soft glow and clinked together in her hands as she wrapped them in flannel cases. The fine glasses and our best Limoges and Haviland china were packed away, to be rolled out in barrels and hidden in the woods. Mother and Charlie worked late at this, and then she packed a bag with essentials and we went to bed wondering what would become of us.

Three in the morning can be very dark, and a candle hardly manages a flicker of light to dress by. The hurried call, "Quickly, we must go now," heard in half-sleep, brings a clutch at the heart and a groping for balance. Pulling on a stocking in the dark, forgetting hair bows; a dress on backward, a sleeve twisted and an arm stuck—no giggles this time—"Hurry, we must go now."

The slow sound of a horse walking on the gravel path

says someone is bringing the animals. The parrots in their cages mutter softly, "Loro, lorito." Their bright yellow and green eyes know that we go in haste, and all the hushed orders say that we must also go in silence.

Most of the villagers had already been scattered. There were only Bartolo and Francisco to help us with the horses. Francisco, just as thin and solemn as Bartolo was chunky and smiling, stood anxiously by to see that stirrups were right. He had come to us from another finca only recently and had already seen too much.

Charlie stood silently in the doorway, his hands folded inside his black silk sleeves. He would not leave. He declared personal war on anyone who rode against San Leandro. "They sit down jail one year!" he threatened; and we couldn't help but smile at each other, for there would be nothing left of them to sit down jail even six months if Charlie got a chance at them with the battery of weapons he had assembled.

All these things were imprinted on my mind and heart, a tableau of our unity as the storm gathered that might separate us all.

Riding out like that gives a strange coldness to the back of your neck. Always people have fled thus into the night, away from their homes, fear sitting out there beyond them in the dark. Perhaps men will always have to run from men, but however often it is done, each time there will be the same intense, still, kind of excitement, the same sudden love of home and what is left behind; for there may be no returning.

We went up the trail toward the mountains, toward the limekiln, and there was a last fragment of moon in the sky. The darkening of the moon was portentous; the limekiln was a dangerous place to go at night—these were omens in which some believed. Secretly I blamed Don Lencho's witchcraft for all the fear that came to us. And I kept thinking, as we rode in the dark wet forest, "If Don Lencho went away, we would be all right again."

For two days we rode over the mountains toward Tumbalá, putting up the first night in a quickly made shelter, riding next morning out of the jungle into sparse high mountain timber, the trail zigzagging down over limestone outcropping. It was a hard journey, and the horses went lame on the rocky trail. All the way I looked for the Karivís, but there were no signs of them anywhere and I was too miserable to ask Papa if he had seen them.

At the free Indian village of Tumbalá we were treated with curiosity and kindness. We slept in hammocks in the cacique's house, a clean native hut with new white pomoy walls that stood beside a stony stream where the water from the mountain was clear and cold. It was a pretty enough village, the huts like mauve mushrooms settled in the green grass of a high mountain meadow.

Mother tried to make us feel that this was adventure, and she managed a gay picnic kind of atmosphere, but our hearts were heavy. Staying like that in the mountain village, seeing the people about their own way of living, would ordinarily have seemed exciting and new. But now, with the sense of having had to run from our own place, it was only distressing.

Two days after we got to Tumbalá, Mariano came for us. He said the bandits had passed around our finca and gone Tipitán way. It might be weeks or months before they came back, and perhaps meantime Father could get some federal troops to come and stay for a time at San Leandro.

We rode home, coming down the last stretch of mountain

175

in the early morning, the sun slowly moving along the slopes behind us, shadows retreating into the canyons as though they were being drawn by some invisible hand into the secret places of the earth. By ten o'clock we rode out into the warm welcome of the finca, where Charlie, undisturbed, was preparing baking powder biscuits with six eggs, especially for our coming.

We unpacked our things gaily enough, and that night played and sang and made plans for Christmas. But the village remained nearly deserted for a week, the people slowly filtering back from hiding, carrying with them a kernel of fear that all our gaiety could not dispel. And refugee families began coming to us again as they had during the revolution, telling stories of violence, hinting, always hinting, that a moment would come when we would be the victims.

Early in December, when the rains were done and spring was flowering the mountain with yellows and dark reds and purples, we rode down to Palenque to stay with Don Ernesto and get some facts. He had a good story to tell.

The capitán, who had now promoted himself to coronel, had arrived in a great whoop at Palenque town. There were only about three hundred people in the village, and there wasn't much to loot in a thatched-hut town like that. So he camped outside, getting the lay of the land and investigating the possibilities of the plantations nearby.

One night the dogs at San Juan finca began to bark. Half-asleep and in his nightshirt, Don Ernesto leaped from bed and raced out of the house, yelling for his armed men to come and help him. Of course he had no armed men, in fact at that time there were only two vaqueros on the place.

His wife, suddenly discovering that he had gone without his rifle, snatched it off the wall, and in her long-sleeved billowing night-dress, her braids flying out behind, went running after him shouting in English, "Ernesto, your rifle!" This woke up the children, who began to scream, and the animals of the place joined in to make a tremendous uproar as effective as the Musicians of Bremen. Don Ernesto roared with laughter as he told us, teasing his wife for rushing out in her nightgown.

"It was she that scared them off," he said, twinkling his eyes at her, "better than ten armed men! Anyhow, all the coronel's men turned and disappeared up the hill, and we were left in peace for the moment."

Evidently the men reported a formidable situation to the coronel, for the bandits rode away from Palenque and didn't return for several weeks. By then Don Ernesto was ready for them. He had called in all his workmen and brought others down from Santa Ysabel, so there were a good number around the place when the coronel came with his contingent. Luckily they were sober, but the coronel was full of swagger. He demanded food for his men and ordered that everything of value about the place be given to him. Don Ernesto met him with broad smiles.

"Welcome to my house, General!" he exclaimed. "I have heard much about you. Delighted to have you for a guest." He promptly offered a pasture for the men to camp in and said he would send beans and tortillas to them, but invited the "general"—now promoted from coronel by the beaming Don Ernesto—to lodge in his own house.

"It would never do for you to camp out there. We have a poor enough place, but you must stay in our house, of course." And with blandishments and much shaking of hands and loud orders for the comfort of the general, Don Ernesto ensconced him and a few "officers" in the ranch house, listened to their bragging, and flattered them to their ears.

Finally, with regrets, they were ready to leave. Don Ernesto said sadly that of course, since they were men of honor, they would realize that it was a great expense to feed two hundred men. The general and his officers were guests and must not think of paying, but they would naturally want to reimburse him for the expenses involved with his army. The general paid, and quite handsomely too.

Father and Don Ernesto, sitting on the porch, roared with joy over the whole situation. It was probably the only case on record of bandits touching nothing, harming no one, and paying for what they got besides.

But that wasn't all the story. There was another encounter that was not so pleasant, but much more satisfactory. This took place at Don Ernesto's small store in the town of Palenque. The building had two doors in front, with a wide porch and benches. Inside there were a single long counter and a door that led to a small storeroom, which had an exit to the rear.

When the bandits returned to Palenque, Don Ernesto was ready for them. They roared into town in regular style. Galloping or at a dead run, hats on the backs of their heads, pistols banging in all directions, they rushed up to the wide porch and pulled to a sudden stop. They leaped or rolled out of their saddles, depending on their state of drunkenness, and poured into the store. Only one front door stood ajar; the other was securely locked. In the storeroom the boys were hustling cases of liquor and gasoline and car-

178

tridges out the back way. They carried them in relays down to the stream, put the liquor and gasoline in the water under some rocks, and hid the cartridge boxes in the brush.

Meantime Don Ernesto handed out drinks in the store, doling out the aguardiente cup by cup. The signal finally came that all was clear. Then, pretending to go to the storeroom for more liquor, he went out, carefully shut and locked the back door, circled around to the front door, and slammed and locked it.

The small store with its galvanized-iron roof was an oven in the midst of a tropic day, even with all the doors open. Closed and crowded with drunken, sweating men, it became a seething, howling inferno. The bandits began fighting each other and pounding on the doors, but Don Ernesto leaned serenely against one with his gun ready, and half the villagers, fully armed, stood by the other.

Don Ernesto finally managed to get word to the leader inside that he would make a bargain. He would let the men out, one by one, but they had to hand over their guns first. With the village men propped against the door to keep the bandits from bursting it open, pistols and rifles were tossed out one by one. Then the men themselves were released, bleary-eyed and full of hate. But they were too drunk to really comprehend what was happening, and most of them passed out on the grass in front of the store. Their teeth had been pulled for the time being, as Don Ernesto put it, though everyone knew they would thirst for revenge of some sort.

We felt sure that revenge would be slow to come. The band was broken up, and until they could get guns and horses again, the scare was over. Meanwhile we were free from worry.

179

We rode back to San Leandro the next day to find that the priest had come, the mule train was in, Charlie had baked "plum pie" with prunes sent by our aunts in California, and Christmas was only a week away.

CHRISTMAS CAME to San Leandro with brightening stars and cool days full of sunshine. At night we drew the big curtains across the porches and were glad of blankets. Chill winds blew in, and even though the thermometer sometimes read eighty when we went to bed, there were mists in the canyons and we were cold.

An excitement came to the plantation in these days, the kind of excitement and expectation that couldn't be explained. It wasn't the boxes that had come from the United States that weren't to be opened until Christmas. It wasn't the plans we laid or the wreaths we made of silver and red-and-green paper, of green leaves and bright flowers. They were part of the excitement, but they weren't it. It was a secret sort of thing that began when branches of sweet-smelling cedar were brought in from the high ranges near Guatemala; when men, stooped under cedar and pine, spread the fragrance of the high forests on the floors of every house. It flickered its promise in the hundreds of little candle flames that gleamed in corners, yellow

181

against dark, redolent green. Surely everyone knows that the gift is not the thing that lies inside the package.

There was excitement for other reasons too. With the priest there, the village was in a state of seething activity. Weddings that had been postponed for two years took place, the couple holding one child and another hanging to the mother's skirts. Christenings were held, with great flourishes and much exchanging of white dresses and veils for the babies and little girls.

Two years was a long time for the village to go unvisited by a priest, and the confessions were long and often loud. Wailing Indian voices admitted pagan sins and violations of all ten commandments to Blessed Mary, Ever Virgin. None of them had seemed important until this moment. But now, under the exhortations of the priest to examine consciences, there came a sudden urge to confess all, and the padre suspected that in the need to be in the limelight some things were embellished to make them more exciting.

True, Feliciana had stolen baby chicks from under the hen of Jerneveva, but Jerneveva had persisted in flirting with Feliciana's husband, and what was a woman in such a position to do? And as for Manuel, yes, he had been with his uncle's wife, but afterward he had tried to hang himself. Nobody could say that he hadn't observed the amenities. It wasn't his fault that they cut him down before he was quite dead. Of course it was really too bad that, since he had lived, his uncle thought he had to hang himself too, but after all he had suffered only a badly swollen throat and hadn't been able to eat for a week. It had really turned out very well, and since no one was complaining now, why discuss it?

The priest took his meals at our table, and we children were owl-eyed with solemnity. He was from Spain, and the "colonies," as he called Mexico, were a special anguish to him. His Andalusian Spanish was full of half-lisping, shushing sounds, his large gray eyes were sad in a long, narrow face, and he talked vehemently about his ideas.

"How can you possibly make any kind of Christians of people like these?" he asked dolefully, his pale hands plucking nervously at his napkin.

He and Father sat long hours discussing morals and philosophy. At first I thought that perhaps he was a saint. Then I decided he could not be, for although saints were supposed to suffer, I had an idea that if they were really touched by the Holy Spirit, they would be serene and full of an inner joy and would know there was something more important than whether they lived in Spain or the "colonies"; whether the people knew Roman Latin or whether they chanted the litany in provincial Spanish. If they were saints they would know that God had come close to them, and that would be a blessing wherever they went. As it was, the villagers accepted him for a man of their religion, but no more. Spaniards in any form they hated, and in the midst of their trust was mistrust. When his three days were up he rode out of the finca, only too glad to be on his way.

The altar where the priest had said mass, baptized children, and held weddings, was turned into a crèche. Hung with bright ribbons, it was populated by clay cows with horns made from the thorn bush, elaborate plaster-of-Paris angels, and a carved wooden Joseph and Mary dressed in Tzeltal dark blue and embroidered huipil. The little figure of Christ had a Chamula hat, and the crib was strung with magenta ribbons. There were candles and figurines and framed pictures of saints, and seeds and charms, and a careful pile of corn in the center.

Each night a lilting sort of melody came up from the village—the faint tink, tink, of small marimbas. Sometimes a guitar wove a softer pattern of sound into the silence and everyone stopped to listen. But when the drums beat and a voice sang the high, wailing, tuneless chants of the hills, even the murmur of cicadas was stilled.

Boys on ladders began stringing Japanese lanterns across the finca in swaying lines of buoyant color, and Mother began planning Christmas dinner. She made fondant, dipping the white candy into chocolate that came from the cacao that grew in the forest. The wild cacao from the hills was the richest, and for days after a picking we had hot chocolate to drink—dark, red-black chocolate with little circles of cocoa oil floating on top. There was milk to go with it, of course, but we didn't use it. We drank our chocolate the way the natives did, with water, or sometimes with pinole and ground cinnamon sticks.

Mother sent our Christmas menu, decorated with a seal of green and red holly, in lieu of Christmas cards to friends and relatives. Thus she indulged in a gentle irony for those "at home" who were eating plum pudding and feeling sorry for us (so their letters said) because we were in such a wild place.

The menu, which included beef soup, tomato and lettuce salad (from Mother's and Charlie's well-guarded garden), mashed potatoes, café noir, and agua sin hielo (because, of course, there was no ice to put in the water), made a feature of turkey à la peacock. That meant we were eating wild pheasant. The beans à la nacionales were black

184

Mexican beans, the prune pie à la Mother-in-law meant that the prunes came from the family ranch in California, and the filberts à la Mauser bullets meant that they were picked in our own woods and dried in the tropic sun. At the bottom Mother added:

Libertad, Constitución, y Independencia,
Viva la República Mexicana!
Viva el Señor Presidente!
Hands across the sea.

At dawn one morning a drumbeat began, slowly at first. It was an imperious voice saying, "Come, come, *come, come!*" It was direct, unhurried, calling. The next night, softly, other drums (bare hands on taut deerskins) began muttering in the dark of the houses. The beat took on a varied meaning, still unhurried, still imperative, still calling, but moving now forward, now back, with a lift to it that made us step high when we walked.

That day, too, the orchestra came in from Salto de Agua, riding on mules, carrying their horns and violins and drums on their saddles. The biggest drum and the bass viol came on Chamula back, held by tumplines across the bearers' foreheads, and everyone shouted advice. "Look out for the tree down across the trail. There's a branch that might punch a hole in the drum!" Up over the rough, muddy trail came the maestro too, riding serenely on a mule, with a city hat on and a formal suit in a satchel on his pommel.

Each day more people arrived—relatives of our workmen, friends, strangers, drifting in from as far as fifty miles away, coming for the big feast days at San Leandro. They came single file out of the woods, whole families, women and children and dogs, moving one by one into

185

the village from the dark trails, until suddenly the pastures were filled with camps of them. Small supper fires blinked red in the night, polka-dotting the wide expanse of San Leandro with little beacons where folk sat and talked.

Through all this we woke and slept and ate and moved to the roll and swish, to the donk, rrrrump-TA-donk of the drums, until two days before Christmas we chased the devil out of town. He was an elegant diablo in red underwear, and he carried his long, forked tail over one arm, brandishing a pitchfork as he pranced about. For a week we had the devil with us, wandering in and out of houses, pestering with petty maliciousness, knocking over pots, and tickling babies' feet. During the course of that week he went into every house, and came out with shrieks and pots flying after him. Chased from pillar to post, he reciprocated by running in front of the horses on horse-racing day, suddenly lassoing a runner on foot-race day, and entering into the chase for the greased pig to the confusion of everything. Sometimes it was hard to tell just who won the races, or whether anyone won them, because when the devil appeared prancing and chortling, everyone dropped everything and went after him, men, dogs, women, and children, all yelling and whooping. Oh, it was a giddy time, and the best of it was that although everyone knew he was one of our own men, their peculiarly Mayan approach to symbolism made it possible for them to completely forget the man and see only the symbol, and who doesn't enjoy a poke at the devil? Personal animosity was kept out of it.

The devil meanwhile had free run of the place, as he had every year, and his machinations knew no limits. He was official and protected; he got into whatever mischief

186

he could, and sometimes he succeeded in an astonishing amount of it. For example, in many a fall there was born a child who strangely resembled the devil of the previous Christmas. But since the man was never held accountable for what the symbol did, and since the woman after all must have had something to do with it, the child was accepted in the family and even looked upon with a sort of whimsical pride. If it was a boy it was usually named Saturnino or some such. It was difficult to know which was considered the more notable crime, the spilling of a pot of beans (precious food) or the reincarnation of the devil nine months later.

The devil's immunity, however, never permitted the man enacting him to take personal revenge, and even his most hated enemies enjoyed a sort of safety from him during his devilship. As a matter of fact, it was usually his best friend who received the crown of horns.

Other strange beings roamed our midst during those days. Tall, thin Francisco, with pillows (two of them) stuffed behind and amplitude attached to his front, walked about in swinging skirts and long black curls, twitching his shoulders. The steatopygia of his rear was out of proportion to his long, thin body, but it undulated and waggled as he minced about in rhythm to the continuous rrrrump-TA-tump of the drums. It was never quite clear who he was supposed to be. Since a general masquerade was in order, a rooster and a hen also wandered about, human except for the enormous chicken masks that rested on their shoulders. They paused from time to time to do the old dance of the rooster and the hen and set everyone to clapping and singing. For a while we even had an owl, who set himself up in a macabre business of making ghoulish charms for children, but in a fit of jealousy the devil broke the owl's head one day and revealed Don Lencho.

Finally, in the midst of the quiet morning of the twenty-fourth, a shriek and a flying stick followed by general hilarity brought everybody running. Out of a back door rushed the red figure, down through the fruit trees toward the river, Lucia and I hanging onto the top of the corral fence to see the chase. Around and in and out of the village rushed the devil, the whole place a bedlam of whooping hilarity.

At last he was cornered by the bodega, where the people in a frenzy of glee tore off his clothes and sent him howling away in mock disgrace, with only a serape to cover his nakedness. Amid shouts of triumph and a mad rush, his red suit, horns, and tail were stuffed with straw, hung on a pole, paraded about town, and finally burned—a wild red effigy dangling in the wind, firecrackers bursting out of its flaming sides.

The fun was over, and the time of the feast began. A steer was killed and barbecued whole, hung from poles in the old way, watched and turned by men specially appointed to do so. The village men stood and watched and argued and gave out advice, and the women made tamales and special dressings for the meat—sage and cumin and orégano and cebollino and alusima, perejil and a dozen other herbs that grew to hand in everyone's garden. And now came the celebration, the candlelight procession and the songs and the slow beat of the music in the bandstand.

On Christmas Eve there was a dance, a wonderful dance in the copal and cedar fragrance of the casa nueva, where

188

all the rubber-pressing implements and the smelly chemicals had been cleared away. Flute and drum and a strange little harp that stood on three legs before the player were orchestra for this. There was heel-thumping, and always the lift in sound that raised your feet off the ground and brought your head up. Soft and loud, loud and soft, the music sang, and the women danced with expressionless faces and easy swaying bodies.

Somebody began shuffling feet in a different rhythm, the dance stopped, and men ran with planks to cover over the big curing pit. Then the zapateo began, thumping out its own violent timing. Men and women stamped two and two on the vibrating boards, feet moving swiftly, heel against heel, heel against board, knees bent, bodies straight, faces solemn and empty of expression. Once in a while a man cracked down with a double stamp of the heel, bringing his foot up high and doubling back his leg behind him to whack down again the harder and twirl around the solemn girl. Then a shout went up with the "Ya-*heeeeee!*" of the Mexican ranchero cry, and broad grins broke out on the dancers' faces. The boards vibrated, the feet stamped, the music jigged endlessly, and the bodies lifted up and down stiffly, shoulders high, knees bent.

Near midnight began the dance of the virgins. Lucia and I sat on one side and watched enchanted, for this was a whirling dervish of a dance, a drawing of girls into the charmed circle, a casting of them out; the male bird in bright plumage choosing a drab mate. Bartolo, in white blouse, white trousers, and bright red sash, danced barefooted in the center, his feet and heels thumping the staccato of the beat. He used his feet on the loose boards like marimba sticks, and as he danced the girls moved in a slow circle around him, their rebozos drawn shyly over their heads and faces, with only wide, luminous eyes to give away the intensity of their excitement. These were the unmarried girls, and one by one Bartolo pulled them into the center, dancing with each for a moment, first back to back, then whirling around her, gyrating, posturing, and leaping, with the boards clapping under his flying feet. Then meekly she went out of the circle, to wait on one side for her turn in the second half of the dance.

We did not see this second half, for excitement was running too high and Mother decided it was time for us to go. The crowded, green-hung hall with its audience of eight hundred or more solemn, watching faces, candlelit faces with shadows flickering over them, suddenly came out of its silence and began to shout and move about. Mother pulled quickly at our sleeves and said, "Come." Someone was pouring out the Christmas drink of fermented corn, and the chanting was growing into a pulsing murmur. The people were forgetting their Spanish and beginning to call out in Chol, Bachajón, Chamula, Tzendal, Tzotzil—shouting out tribal calls, the wailing, keening ceremony for the wrongs of the world, and the quickened beat and salute to the good and the new.

Hustled to the house and tucked into hammocks on the porch of the casa grande where we could watch, we fell asleep until the last dancing was done. Then, awakened by the people pouring out of the pavilion and the joyous thumping and tootling of the band in the bandstand, we watched the whole village full of laughter, enchanted with itself and its celebration. Somewhere in all of it there was a memory that this was the birthday of Christ; but the songs were ancient ones, chanted by the people of Maya

190

long before Christ was known to the Eastern world, and the name of Itzamná, the Christ-figure of their old faith, grew and grew until it was first on their lips.

Watching from the porch, we became a vicarious part of the whole—the lights, the voices, the feeling that went into the laughter and the chants. Ave Maria, Here the Newborn Christ the Lord, and Itzamná who was the sacred gift of Hunab Ku with his hands full of a myriad zontlis of eloti, the new corn—they were all mixed together somehow, until it was not very clear in my mind why there were differences in the names, for creation was God's; and if Itzamná had brought the new corn, and Christ had blessed it, and both had talked of the brotherhood of man, who could deny one for the other?

So Christ and Itzamná were sung down the village in a great chant that grew and grew until a procession was formed. The people moved with torches about the village, visiting this house and that, giving the old calendar of happenings, giving the ancient signals of the coming of a sacred one, and in the same moment making crosses in the doorways and hanging gilded stars on the wrists of the children. It was mixed up, but it didn't seem to matter at all, for in it was a memory that somewhere there was a will to good, the bondad de Dios, if men could forget themselves and find it.

At three in the morning, when the flares had died down, a careless torch set fire to one of the Japanese lanterns. Suddenly the bright flame caught in a wind and whirled lantern after lantern into red ginger flowers in the night. In the midst of the feet running to save them, a greater shout was raised. The bodega! It was on fire too. Half the world was ablaze.

191

When the black smoke and the leaping dark red fire were done, the story was told over and over, by each who had seen it first, by each who had helped pull Marcelina reeling and giddy drunk out of the blazing building, by each who had seen the spilled aguardiente. For Marcelina, in an excess of good will, had broken open the supply of spirits and was passing out drinks to all and sundry. But it wasn't only aguardiente she handed out. Bolts of cloth and kilos of rice and beans and scissors and mirrors and other things were given until she lurched against a lantern, so they said, and knocked it over and burned the whole place down.

So that Christmas morning the question was again raised in San Leandro as to whether a man should beat his wife. There were those who said that only a beating would give a woman proper respect for her man. But Domotilo, who once had given a beating to Marcelina, stood sadly at the casa grande door and said he would assume the debt but could not beat her, and Father fully approved. Marcelina was sent for a temporary visit to her family in Tipitán, and Father reluctantly started Domotilo on an extra hour of work a day.

All the finca rocked with the scandal—until it was learned that Don Lencho had been in the bodega, had poured the first aguardiente, and had finally been the one who knocked over the lantern. So the debt of Domotilo was crossed off and Don Lencho was put to work. Peace once more settled on our village; Marcelina swished across the green common in her full pink skirt, and a new bodega of stone and mortar was built.

Witch doctors are not given to work, however, and it wasn't a month before Don Lencho suddenly had a call

192

to make an incantation in another village. He left, his alligator pouch bulging with dried lizards and other trappings. The new red ribbons that bound his wrists and the purple headband were contributed by Marcelina, who wanted no pins in her effigy.

Thus Christmas was celebrated among us; and that year, with the beginning of Twelfth Night celebration, the Karivís came down from the mountain and made their new fire under the ceiba tree.

HERE IS A TIME toward the
end of childhood when one goes around a corner and over
a stile, and then nothing looks quite the same again. The
child discovers himself and loses the universe.

By some mysterious grace, the Karivís kept a simplicity,
a purity if you like, in their approach to the world. Things
were not for liking or disliking; identification with self
was no part of their concept. Choice was a matter of
custom and taste, criticism almost unheard of. "One" did
things, not you or I, for they saw the world in a wholly
impersonal way. There were no judgments, only decisions
where your own acts were concerned. If a thing appealed
to you, you were warm to it, flowed toward it. If it didn't,
you removed yourself either physically or by withdrawing
your awareness. They accepted the world in which they
found themselves, not bleakly or with resignation, but
with an assumption that it existed "as is" and was a vast
potential miracle.

Their ability to evaluate the important and discard the
unnecessary was profound and peaceful. But with it strode

194

an almost fierce delight in unveiling the face of eternity, in "catching the glance of God," as they put it. Each day was a completely new experience, as though the sun had never risen before. A red-mottled bug walking up the slope of a green pea—not its structures as seen through a microscope, not the hows and whys of its behavior, but IT—was to them an apparition, a strange wandering thing, a fragment of the universe. Their personal desires or sorrows could not cloud their ability to see objectively. They seemed to see with a dual focus, as if they were watching two performances going on at the same time, the one in their inner being and the other in the world outside. Perhaps they looked upon themselves with the same astonishment and amused curiosity as that with which they saw the bug. But the key to all they taught me was an awareness that there was more to a temple than the stones that built it.

Their careful preservation of the past, in spite of the few ways in which they were able to serve it, was a part of their reverence for the "force that built the temple"; and ritual was an experience, an attention absolute and listening, to a principle beyond human analysis—as though through ritual they could silence heart and mind and body, and hear beyond their own existence.

In the short years I knew them, the Karivís tried to keep this dimensional duality in me, teaching me slowly, fixing me with an attention deliberate and demanding, so that I felt an urge upon me, like a hunger, to absorb all I could. The jungle, so completely nonhuman nature, and the Karivís with their human culture, possessed me beyond all other things, and I became a thread woven back and forth between them and the modern world.

195

The simple daily life of the plantation, the direct Christian teaching of my father, the guidance of my mother, and the Oriental concepts of Charlie were a background for a way of life. But, more powerful than anything else, the jungle and the Karivís were realities that worked directly on my thinking.

I experienced the entirety and the individual features of our jungle as separate things; the specific and the general were not always related in any way. Snakes were a specific. A bird, *a* tree, were completely different from TREE or BIRD, the representative whole. There were also things like the chi cheng trees or fever trees, which were specifics in a place like "black jungle," which was an absolute. If it were necessary to clear a part of the jungle where there were chi cheng trees, great care had to be taken in cutting them down, because one drop of their sap contained enough acid to burn great blisters on the skin or to blind the eyes. But different sections of the forest had their own over-all personalities, and we spoke of "open jungle," "black jungle," or "old forest" not so much because of their difference in growth, although that had something to do with it of course, as because of the moods we found in different heavily grown areas. These moods sometimes changed, and from time to time what had been a good place altered with a passing uneasiness, and we kept away.

In all but black jungle I felt a tremendous love, as though no worldly danger could reduce the beauty to a condition of jeopardy for me. How much of this came from the forests themselves and how much from the Karivís' ability to create this awareness in me I do not know, but it was hard to understand why others did not feel safe and happy in the woods as I did.

As I grew from childhood toward adolescence, I was permitted to go with Father up the mountain to the Kariví karival, a group of villages, of places where they spent certain seasons of the year. Since they almost never stayed from year to year in the same houses, the groups of buildings were not technically villages. Their moving about did not come from nomadism, for they considered the old ruined cities of Maya as their real centers; but each year they had to make new pottery and new roofs, so they simply made new houses as well in a place they felt was better "this year."

There were hundreds of untracked jungle mountains for them to move about in, but except for the pilgrimages that took the priests to all the known places of ancient worship once every nine years, each group of Karivís stayed in a given area. Once another body of them came over the mountain and stayed with those who lived near us on Don Juan. That was the year the puberty rites were held near the white limestone scar on the face of the high mountain, where stone temples lay crumbled under the jungle trees.

At the beginning of their adolescence, the Kariví children I had seen and occasionally played with suddenly became shy, and slowly I began to be separated from them. In those times when we were together, when they were camped outside the finca or when I went with Father up the mountain beyond the limekiln, I learned to use their language and understand what they meant. Friendship with them was a kind of enchantment, all the more absorb-

197

ing because my times with them were rare. The sudden difference in them and their growing shyness toward me brought a hurt I could not understand. I reached out to stay with and be part of them and learn the things they were to learn, but more and more I was left behind in a curious way. For the first time I felt a striking sense of desolation, a cruel sort of discrimination that was in no way eased by the fact that it was unintentional. I simply could not go where they went, because my skin was too white and another culture claimed me.

What was I to do with the things I had become a part of, how reconcile myself to being what I was not allowed to be in the world of the other humans I knew? How could I cease to be one with the forest and the earth and the tropic sky, the violent sunsets and sinister dawnings, the mauve and saffron of the momentary twilights, the damp, hot fecundity of summer jungle, the cool of its rivers, the pale green sheaths of new banana leaves after rain? These things were not things seen or felt, but part of my very self. And the people, who were my people in a curious way—how could I deny them or their way of life? I was part of them too, and yet never quite of them. Never to belong, to remain on the periphery of the Karivís' world, was a strange relationship. So I could only watch when the puberty rites began, although I had shared in some of the training.

The Karivís tried to help me understand what was expected of one in the transition from child to adult, but I could not take part in all the mystery of their learning, or stand with their girl children in the bathing pool being taught how a woman's body is. I could not sleep under their roofs to listen, half-awake, half-asleep, to the songs

198

of the old women telling over and over the meaning of newness, of oldness, of seeds deep in the earth; the meaning of the upward sweep of a coconut palm, what a curve signified and why it was a poem, what a straight line was and why it was a shout.

I heard them talking of these things, and Caiya Uum taught me in fragments, and once I went with them to the pool below the rapids.

Kariví girls from ten years on lived apart in a group being taught to become women. The boys began their training to be men at eleven years, and the training karivals were separated by at least the village's length. Since the settlements were usually arranged in a line along a riverbank or in a semicircle around a lake, the karivals at either end were sometimes more than a mile apart. During the mornings the children were at home, helping with the very real everyday needs of the family, but with afternoon they went into seclusion, where they stayed until dawn the next morning. What was done in the karivals no one ever said, for these things were not talked about; there was no reason to do so, as they had been experienced by every man and woman grown. It was a secret time, and only once, there at the pool, was I included.

The River San Leandro was a high mountain stream, coming directly out of the great inner caverns of Don Juan. It rushed clean and burbling white over the limestone into a pool shaded by wapake and caoba trees, edged with tree ferns. Blue clay and white limestone bordered the pool, and there transparent fish moved in a liquid as clear and cool as air. To swim there was like being in a green jade vase, with the sky above caught and held in the water.

That afternoon was hot. We floated face down, staring

199

at the fish and fresh-water snails. Our bottoms rose into the warm air like round floats on a Japanese fish net. We were children nearly ready to become women; and with that peculiar sensitiveness that comes at such a time, when we came up, staring at each other with water-blurred eyes, we knew that something had happened to us. With one accord we paddled to old Na Ná, who sat under the wapake on the bank. How children and creatures know these things no one can say. She had called us without saying a word, and we had heard her and come.

We lay half in and half out of the water, splashing with our feet, our chemises clinging to us wetly while we waited for something to happen.

A young woman, her long black hair floating out on the water, swam to us and said, "Look."

We stopped splashing and watched her lift water in her hands, letting it trickle slowly into the pool again. Then she put her hands, fingers spread, into the water; and, moving them slowly, she began a low singsong mesmeric chant:

Water is the first great mystery. It goes where you cannot go, but is part of all of you. It is the sign of women—it and the moon. It is soft and cool and has virtue. It brings health where it touches. Like women there is nothing on earth more hideous if it is fouled, because it is made for healing and beauty.

Then after a few minutes, raising her arms to point up toward the mountain, she added, "The five fingers of the gods of rain made the first rivers, and you play in the first waters of the five."

We touched the water and held it in our hands and felt its silky coolness. Then suddenly, with a quick self-conscious look at me, the children plunged into the pool and

200

paddled to the other side. I stood on the blue clay bank, watching them go, left behind, knowing that I could not follow.

They climbed out on the white rocks of the river and ran quickly and in silence into the woods. The young woman followed them, pulling on a hand-woven white and blue refajo and tying back her hair. Slowly I went to float in the water alone, and now I sensed that somehow it held me differently. It touched all of me, and I felt the caress of the moving current. In this way I was not as I had been, and in one way I had already changed. But how much more the shy children were to experience there in the shadows of the great trees I was not to know.

So I was taught by small things that were great things, change by change, knowing something I had not known the moment before. And always there was time for the new thing to become part of me, unforgotten, an element of my very nature. In this way the whole pattern of Mayan thinking—that is, recognition of symbolism in all things beyond their corporeal selves—became a gradual and entire approach to living.

The puberty rituals, the ceremonies marking the change from girl to woman, from boy to man, came in those months of the year when sifting rain still kept the jungles wet, when rivers still ran riot with newness over their stones and rumbled down the mountains in violence, thunder caught in water.

Early in March, before burning cornfields and pastures made the forests sick with yellow smoke, before thunderstorms came up out of the lowlands with the heat of April, came the rituals. For months ahead the children had been made ready by the gradual process of instruction, which continued for months afterward. Thus no sudden line of

201

demarcation was drawn, saying, "Now you are this and no longer that." This was a preparation and a growth, and the sanctification of the children into symbolism and mysticism and the use of the world and the world's body for the development of the spirit.

Back in the mountains, back of the limekiln on the trail to the Tumbalá hills, there were ruins. On the ridges of the hills, overlooking the valleys that ran toward the lowlands, were pyramids and buildings of stone, crumbled and covered with jungle. Tremendous trees writhed their roots about ancient stone faces. Like other hidden cities, this was a place of worship still for the Karivís. There each year the puberty rites were held; and there in a courtyard, almost the last time I was with them as a child, the dawn sun slanting red upon the green turrets of the trees, the first rite of puberty took place.

Little girls stand like small totems, motionless, their clean blouses and dark refajos a pattern in blue and white, their faces like little earthen images, their bodies raised up, suspended somehow by the luminous expectancy of their dark eyes.

Little boys, thin, muscle-ribbed, stand solid, eyes heavy-lidded, shading themselves against showing emotion. Their faces are closed to keep secret the new sacred knowing. Their lips, slightly open, wait to speak the new words Caiya Uum will teach them. No twitching or impatience for goodies afterwards. No one stands to sing a song. No one will speak to show his learning. This is no gesture, this is the moment itself. Acceptability. Belonging. No need to prove anything, each knows what he knows.

202

The words of Caiya Uum come in a low chant that touches the gray stones around about and come back to each in soft clear meaning. He first speaks to the girl children, who move slowly, forward and back, as they listen:

Yesterday you were a child. You knew the work of women, building fires, making posole, weaving the cloth to cover your family and yourselves. Yesterday you were a child. Now you have moved into the time of longing, of need, of desire. Where is the end of your world, and what do you find there? Sing your song, girl children; sing it, weave it into a chant day and night, and make of it a great question that will not have its answer until you have been loved by man, borne his children and fed them, wept over them, and become old.

The children move slowly, forward and back, and the new sun turns light on the gray stone. The madrugada is past and morning begins. The girls sing, monotone, oddly, a chorus in a ritual mass:

> *Jahon jalto antz anasto*
> *Scux lejal choc me hu*
> *Antzel nechan*
> *Kahal kin cuhun silel?*
>
> *I am daughter of the moon,*
> *Child of the jungle,*
> *Sister of the sea;*
> *The sun is my brother*
> *But who is my lover?*

They begin to dance slowly, a voluptuous movement already not strange to the newly formed bodies, a rhythmic lifting of feet and a bending forward, pantomime of worship, stylized grinding of corn, of making love, of holding the newborn. Then they pull thin, veil-like rebozos over their faces, to show that the mystery of being a woman is still hidden in the days to come.

> *Spisil ya shu yahun pasel*
> *Oncan in tael*
> *Johoncan in tael*
> *Nijunuc chulel canvil.*

> *Omnipotence*
> *I wait, I wait,*
> *Who, for my soul's love?*

And Caiya Uum answers them:

Born in mystery, old before you were born, given wisdom and danger of your wisdom, given power and softness and generosity, hands for good and lips for evil, you will lift men up in their babyhood, help their stumbling feet, grow them into men, and then destroy them if you can; for it is a god you have dreamed of, not a man. And when this man who is not a god has touched you and found the secret of yourself, you will be bound to him, wounded by him; and you will wait on him. You will take his caresses and his abuse, you will crawl at his feet when he hurts you, worshiping the god in him and plotting the death of the man. For when you are an old woman he will quiver before your

204

tongue and will shrink before the measurement of him in your eyes. This women were born into, this their greater sorrow, their greater glory. For they must be loved by man, remembering in their souls how it was to be loved by angels. Return to your angels, worship them still, nor give your love, but only your tenderness and your laughter, to the child and half-god who is man.

The small girls move back and back into the cool shadows behind the high stone pillars, behind the great swinging censers of clay marked with the month glyph and puberty glyphs and the sacred signs of life and Itzamná. Incense pours forth in blue pungence, a vapor of odor to envelop them. Caiya Uum moves quickly to them with a sharp black obsidian knife. He cuts the cord that hangs about each girl's waist, the cord that suspends the bead of amber or of jade that has hung there since birth. The beads are scattered under hurrying feet, never to be picked up again. The girls are gone, and with them their childhood, and they run, run like frightened deer-children on noiseless feet.

The little boys shuffle their feet. Their eyes are half-closed; they look out warily upon a world they do not know. Then comes the chant of the new words:

> *I am the son of men*
> *Not gods.*
>
> *I have no mystery,*
> *Only truth.*

205

Truth that is sorrow
For man.
I walk alone.
I want to be God.
I am not.
I have power.
I have humility.
I wait to be told what I shall be told.
I shall hear with vision,
I shall see with thunder.
If I betray the gift of my hands
I shall perish.

Caiya Uum lifts the hand glyphs of new-made stucco into place on the wall. Again the story of Itzamná and man, again the ritual of the sacred hand, the gift that man must guard; for if in his stupidity or carelessness he defiles it, this miracle that only Itzamná could bring to earth from God, he has also defiled his soul.

Each hand glyph has a face, a month, and a date, with a separate symbol for each boy, a guide to his destiny as man. Caiya Uum puts them against the wall and fastens them there. The glyph is not a forecast of how each boy's life will be; it is only to teach him how his life should be, to show who his star is, who guides his thoughts, and what symbol is his to live by.

The censers swing high, blue copal smoke pouring from them and making halos in the early sunlight. The boys stand in white breechcloths with magenta tassels, white turbans, and magenta neckcloths, their bodies gleaming golden with sacred oil, their hands outstretched, palms up:

Divine is your hand,
Divinely given.
Yours the eternal search,
Yours the why, power and thrust for the future.

Guard the past, guardians of Maya.
Guard the future, guard the sacred hand.

Caiya Uum puts a flaming coal of copal into each palm, searing the fingers first. Not a face changes, not a hand that flinches.

> *Pain you must know.*
> *Cleanse with pain.*
> *Women are born to pain.*
> *Men must learn it.*

Then follows the phallic ritual of the shedding of blood. Each boy walks past the altar and comes away, his breechcloth red with bleeding, a thorn embedded in his flesh. So, his hand seared, his blood shed, his body pierced with a thorn, he has already learned to feel beyond the pain of his body; to know that blood is the earth's knowing; to remember that his hand is the instrument of his will to create or destroy, that he must keep it the instrument of his spirit.

I had been forgotten. I stood back in the shadows, by a pillar. The women had turned away and were moving in a rhythm of their own to the music of a tlatil. The men sat stolid along the stone steps leading down into the tree-hung courtyard. The boys went away, and Caiya Uum was left standing near the altar chanting softly. All I could hear was the end of every phrase, when he brought his

207

hand down upon the altar and lifted his head upward and then the word came clear: "Itzammá!"

When Na Ná came to take me back to the karival, I had found one of the jade pieces and one of amber, scattered by the hurrying feet of children. I held them out to her, but she pushed my hand away. "Ma yuk" she said, "there isn't any"—meaning that the symbols did not exist any longer. I understood I might keep them. The jade piece I dropped somehow on my way home, but the amber I did not lose.

For a year now, since we had returned from the States, nothing had been quite the same at San Leandro. The constant threat of bandits and a new flux and change in the people themselves were part of the feeling of unrest. Political turmoil continued. Madero had been murdered, and General Huerta sat insecurely in the president's chair. The revolution had made a change in the people's thinking, a loosening of family ties, and had driven rich and poor alike into uncertainty of both morals and mores.

Of our friends, few were left. Don Ernesto carried on somehow, but all the Americans on fincas like Lumija and La Esperanza had departed, and many of the Mexican landowners were destitute. Henich too was gone. His own men had turned against him at last, bound him hand and foot, thrust him head first into a hill of fire ants, and deserted the plantation in a body. By pure chance a party of Federales came by within minutes and fished him out in time. But no one would work for Henich after that, so he was forced to close his finca and get out.

Only a few plantations, like ours, had remained relatively untouched; and among our workmen, many who had come in recent years left to go back to childhood homes, looking for relatives. Some tried the new "freedom," roaming from here to there and trying this work or that. None of the old guard left San Leandro, but many new ones came, and unrest kept them moving.

From the outside world came changes too. There had been a murder at Sarajevo, and Don Ernesto came up to the finca to talk long and hard with Father, sitting out on the porch in the hot nights. He discussed German strength and what might become of Europe under the Kaiser, and they spread maps on the table and moved pins to follow the advances and retreats of the contending armies. They saw signs that the United States might come in too. It seemed to me as if the whole world had lost its balance, had drunk of Don Lencho's chilio brew, and had gone screaming down the highways of Europe, forgetting everything that history had meant.

Father talked with us about it, looking up at the silent stars, squinting one eye and rubbing his hand against his bearded chin. "It's like rabies," he said. "One gets bitten and the whole pack goes off." And he talked of Armageddon. "No telling where it will end now," he added, as if somehow the war were his personal sorrow.

Then there was the rubber market. For some time it had been wavering, dropping lower and lower, and finally one day when the mulada arrived with the mail, Father came in from his office with a tired look in his eyes and a sag to his shoulders. The price of rubber had fallen from five dollars to four cents a pound.

"At that figure we can't pay workmen to collect rubber

and keep up equipment and curing, send it out to the Gulf, and then ship it to New York. I guess we are stumped for a while." But although he spent more and longer hours in his office mulling over reports and wrote many long letters to the States, he did not let us see his real concern and the growing conviction that, temporarily at least, he would have to shut down the plantation.

Standing there at the casa grande looking down the clean sweep of village and woods washed by sun and wind, it didn't seem possible that things wouldn't be all right again. But Mother's sudden illness determined the matter. The doctor took a week to reach us, diagnosed her attack as appendicitis, and urged Father to get her out as soon as possible.

One night at dinner Papa spoke aloud of the decision he finally had to make, leaning back in his chair with his coffee cup in his hand, smiling at us all with his deep blue eyes, as if he knew we would be all right, whatever was to happen.

"Well, girls," he announced, "we are going to send you and your mother back to the States for a while. It's time you went to school so you can get diplomas and go on to college."

Mother and Lucia looked up quickly. I stared down at my plate and then searched Papa's eyes to see if he were really as glad as he sounded. He looked back at me, and we both knew; and I drew some comfort from the knowledge that he was as miserable about it as I.

That night the ceiba tree caught fire. The ceiba was old, so old that it towered head and shoulders above the tremendous forest. Lianas trailed down from its wide-spreading branches, from its high boughs oriole nests swung in the wind and mingled with the crests of other trees. Its trunk and great vine-covered ramifications were gardens of moss and orchids. It stood sentinel for us all across the river by the milpa.

Sparks from a new clearing the men were burning started flames in dried brush near the tree. Once a tree like that started to burn, nothing could stop it. The moss and vines made fuses along which flames crept to the upper branches. In the heat the thick outer bark began to crack and fire worked its way beneath, into crevices and to the tree's core.

In the dark I stood watching, my face pressed against the veranda screen, unable to cry, knowing a hurt and foreboding too dreadful for tears. Sparks flew high into the night, making of my tree a torch against the dark mountain. It was the sacred tree of the Mayans, the best for sheltering man, one natural benevolence in all the impersonal jungle. Between its wide roots I had sat with Caiya Uum. There I had learned to make the little pyramids with the three crosses on top.

I knew the wind would never find the ceiba again, with its lifted branches, green and expectant. And what of the orioles, of the little orange sloths that lived high in the leafy masses of philodendron? I turned my face away from that part of the jungle and fiercely hated the people who had done this thing. More than all, I kept thinking, "Now the Karivís won't have any place to come to, and I no place to meet them."

It took three days for the great tree to be consumed, and its smoke hung like a pall over the finca. On the last night something woke me, and I went to watch in the midnight darkness as the top crumbled and fell, white ash and red glowing coal, down into the forest below. I heard the moan that comes to the jungle when something beloved in it passes, and the high keening of some villagers who kept ceremonies of protection for the spirit of the tree and for themselves. The whole jungle woke with it and shrieked and howled and roared, the endless wailing cry of creatures and man left on earth when a spirit departs. Then like a sigh a small wind blew from the mountain, monkeys coughed down by the river, a bird called away up the canyon, and the night went on about its business of living.

Before morning, lying in bed and staring at the stars that shone into the room, I remembered that the Karivís would say simply, "The wind has changed, Catarina." And indeed it had.

There was much talk of what this change would mean. Through our sadness at leaving there ran an excitement over things to come. Although I couldn't imagine much of it, some of Lucia's eager anticipation caught at me too, and Mother made us feel in a way that we were returning to our own kind. There would be plays and concerts and studies that would put all the world and its wonders into our hands.

"It's a going out," Papa said to us, "an adventure in discovery. There are people and places and things you never dreamed of, Catarina. You know what you know, and if you never forget what you have learned here, nothing will be very fearsome out there."

But I knew he was talking to himself more than to us, and suddenly I felt selfish at being so miserable when the real loss would be his. Here at San Leandro he had taken charge of what was meant to be only a stock-market promotion, and he had made it a rubber plantation of worth

213

—three million dollars' worth over the course of the years. He had loved it from the start, every minute of it—the torrential rains, the heat, the cool of mountain nights, the low fires down village, and the singing that made everything good when the season was done. Out of nothing, against great odds, he had built a kingdom for himself, free in the sun. Now the world he had left was reaching down the long miles to take it away from him. For me the change might be a beginning, but for Father it was a turning away from a manner of life and could well be an end.

At dawn on the day we left Charlie and I clung together a moment, and he reminded me sternly that I must become a great lady like my mother. Then brusquely he went off to stand alone, his hands in his sleeves, a great scowl on his face, while he watched us mount.

It was five in the morning, barely light, when we started out. Mother as always was perfect in her divided skirt, spotless shirtwaist, fringed gauntlets, and high peaked sombrero, and beside her Father, with his cork helmet and boots, was mounted on Gavilán. Lucia had her Blanco to ride, and my black Prieto was ready to carry me away. It seemed just like any other day of riding out. The mules had gone ahead with their loads of trunks and valises and boxes—the wicker and canvas trunk that once had fallen into the river, the streamer trunk that Aunt Mary had taken to Paris, and the little dress trunk she had bought there. Father's books and papers, even some of the parrots in their big metal cages, were strapped on the pack saddles. We would leave the parrots at Don Ernesto's, Mother said.

All the village was standing in front of the houses in the early morning light to watch us go and to give the long halloo of farewell when we turned out through the gate into the jungle. We stopped at the edge of the finca and looked back, a last look and a lift of the arm and hand for our beloved San Leandro. In the late dawn light Don Juan loomed black and brooding, dominating the world. Trails of white mist hovered in the lower canyons, the sky was pale and starless, and the people seemed unreal, like thin cardboard figures before the straight rows of houses.

The casa grande looked as if it were still sleeping, dark and silent. Above it on the rooftree (and we all looked to see) we hoped to find the blue heron, the sign of protection, of our returning, that had never before failed to be there when we rode out. Instead, we saw a white egret. It stood erect, its head lifted, like an alabaster image against the dark trees beyond. Mother cried out and turned half-around in her saddle to stare at it, and Mariano and Bartolo crossed themselves and bowed their heads.

"A white crested heron is an omen of travel," Bartolo said softly as we all looked in silence. Then he added slowly, "But travel of the soul."